Susan Stitt

Susan G. Stitt
70
Co

—The— WORD BOOK

GYLES BRANDRETH

With a foreword by Dr Robert Burchfield CBE

and cartoons by David Colton

 **ROBSON BOOKS**

First published in Great Britain in 1988 by Robson Books Ltd,
Bolsover House, 5–6 Clipstone Street, London W1P 7EB

Copyright © 1988 Gyles Brandreth

Illustrations © David Colton

British Library Cataloguing in Publication Data

Brandreth, Gyles, *1948–*
The word book.
1. English language
I. Title
420

ISBN 0 86051 550 8

Photoset and printed in Great Britain by
Redwood Burn Limited
Trowbridge, Wiltshire

CONTENTS

Foreword 1

Introduction 3

Part One: Word Work 7

Words 9

Wonder Words 37

Old World, New Words 56

Wayward Words 115

Part Two: Word Play 129

Introduction 131

Word Entertainments 132

Word Games 157

Word Puzzles 180

Word Quizzes 193

Solutions to the Word Puzzles 213

Answers to the Word Quizzes 222

Bibliography 227

ACKNOWLEDGEMENTS

In preparing *The Word Book*, and the *Pears Book of Words* on which it is based and which was published by Pelham Books in 1979, I have drawn on all the books in the Bibliography (page 227) and several others, but my principal debt must be to the *Oxford English Dictionary* and especially to its *Supplement* produced under the editorship of Dr Robert Burchfield.

FOREWORD

Gyles Brandreth came up to Oxford University and made his mark in various ways but, as far as I know, was no more than ordinarily interested in the English language at that stage. It wasn't long before he began to write little books on engaging topics: party games (*AA to Zounds Sounds*), dominoes, waiting games ('Waiting for the penny to drop', 'Waiting for inspiration', etc), and so on. He branched out into games like Monopoly, and in a deadly contest in North America played a game with gold dollars or a gold board (I forget which) in a department store window. Games, acrostics, and the like, led inevitably to Scrabble, the parlour game par excellence of the twentieth century, and it was in this context that his path and mine crossed. He organized a National Scrabble Championship on behalf of the manufacturers and, as master of ceremonies, soon showed that he had an enviable ability to keep the knives of the finalists from flashing, by a deft remark about the brevity of life, or on the art of losing with grace, or by some other temper-soothing device. He asked me which dictionary should be used as the final arbiter for all those short, difficult, or rare words so beloved of Scrabble players, and I recommended the *Shorter Oxford*. Because it was not an easy dictionary to use for such a purpose, especially when the finalists were brandishing their challenges, he invited me to act as adjudicator at the National Scrabble Final, and for several years, to my amazement, I found that I actually enjoyed forming rapid judgements on words like *jad, oe, querl, unwooed,* and *zo*. As the games went on I can only surmise that osmosis occurred and my own love of the *Oxford English Dictionary* and of its derivatives infected him too, and the first major result of this process is shown in the pages that follow.

The book is divided into two sections, Word Work (the

serious half) and Word Play (the rest). In the first section he provides a sketch of the evolution of English from the first records until modern times, with, among other things, interesting comparisons of the Lord's Prayer from the Anglo-Saxon version to that of the New English Bible, examples of words which have a continuous history in English from the earliest times to the present day, and of others like OE *niman* (to take) and *wlonc* (proud) that have withered away to be replaced or supplemented by words from other languages, especially French (but also Hungarian, Turkish, Hebrew, etc). He shows more than usual interest in bypaths of the language – very long and very short words, the colourful vocabulary of Lewis Carroll and of P G Wodehouse, proliferating suffixes like *−centric, −cide,* and *−ism,* and the wayward language of those who, with seeming ease, use expressions like 'overall monitored mobility' or 'optimal incremental hardware', and of teachers who talk about 'multimode curricula and empirically validated learning systems'.

The second section dwells lovingly on all those forms of verbal amusement that enable us all to pass an idle hour harmlessly: acrostics, anagrams (a shoplifter = has to pilfer), malapropisms, mnemonics (the initial letters of the words in the phrase '*L*ittle *m*en *i*n *s*hort *b*lack *m*ackintoshes' apparently enables one to remember the names of a frog's arteries), and all kinds of puzzles and quizzes ('There is a fifteen-letter word in which no letter is used more than once. Can you think of it?').

It is a book for every family in the land to savour (Part I) and enjoy (Part II).

ROBERT BURCHFIELD

INTRODUCTION

Communication with a capital C is one of the great cult concepts of our time. But no communication can be achieved in any save the most superficial way without words. A twitch, a wink, a nudge, a kiss, passionate love-making (*bonking* in the new slang), and hitting someone over the head with an iron bar (*bonking* in the old slang), are forms of communication, no doubt, but *real* communication, creative communication, communication that can sustain and uplift and inspire, is only possible with words. Even Trappist monks, vowed to silence, think their prayers in words.

That said, don't worry. This isn't a portentous tome about Communication with a capital C. It's simply a book about words, their origins and history, the ways in which we create and destroy them, use and abuse them, and the vast amount of *fun* that we can have with them.

As you'll have noticed, it is written in English, the mother tongue of 320 million people and the richest of the word's languages, which number over two thousand. The *Oxford English Dictionary* lists some 500,000 English words and the language probably contains half a million technical terms on top of that. The Germans have a vocabulary of 185,000 words. The French have fewer than 100,000, including such notorious examples of *franglais* as *les blujines*, *le weekend* and *le snacque-barre*, which President Pompidou's commission on terminology reluctantly agreed to tolerate, but excluding the 350 like *le hit-parade* and *le zoning* now banned from official use. Peking Chinese – called Mandarin – alone may have a vocabulary to rival that of English, but no other language comes near it.

The English language is rich because it isn't pure. It's a mongrel tongue. Emerson called it, 'the sea which receives tributaries from every region under heaven'. It has taken almost two thousand years to evolve. The Celts, Jutes, Angles, Saxons, Greeks, Romans, Danes, Normans, Dutch, Germans and French (to name but a few) made a major contribution. So did Shakespeare. He coined 1,700 words, *assassinate, suspicious, barefaced, bump, castigate, critical, countless, dwindle, gnarled, hurry, impartial, lapse, laughable, lonely, leapfrog, misplaced* and *monumental* among them. When Lewis Carroll combined *gallop* with *triumph* and came up with *galumph*, he created another. The American writer Gelett Burgess coined *bromide* and *blurb*. Vidkun Quisling, the Earl of Sandwich, General Shrapnel and Captain Boycott actually gave their own names to the language. The First World War contributed *binge, camouflage, cushy, scrounge, umpteen* and *zoom*. The Second World War saw the arrival of *blackout, blitz, boffin, bull-dozer, jeep* and *wishful thinking*.

New words are springing up all the time – *teenager, doddle, commuter, hippie, motel, Muzak, discotheque* and *streaker* for a person rushing naked from point A to point B, a word that managed to travel the English-speaking world in under a week – and old words are always getting new meanings. (The writer Marghanita Laski once concocted a couple of sentences consisting of words with which Jane Austen would certainly have been familiar but not one of which she would have understood in its modern sense: 'After so many Manhattans, better not take hash. But she needed a new face, so she propped up the baby grand and reached for her compact.') To our grandparents the word *gay* had a specific and enchanting meaning. Its modern usage has spoilt the word for many of them.

The fate of *gay* is just the sort of example people cite when bemoaning the decline of the English language. Working on the principle that the fabled past was so much better than the awful present and that nowadays even nostalgia isn't what it used to be, people have been bemoaning the decline and predicting the imminent eclipse of the English language for generations.

Jonathan Swift, the eighteenth-century satirist, was appalled by what the English were doing to their language. He wanted to get rid of such words as *sham, banter, mob, bully* and *bamboozle*, all of which seem rather charming and useful words to me. Dr Johnson, whose famous *Dictionary* appeared in 1755, strongly disapproved of *clever, fun* and *stingy*. Two centuries ago, John Witherspoon, one of the signatories of the Declaration of Independence, a Scotsman who went to America in 1769 to become President of Princeton, grumbled: 'I have heard in this country, in the senate, at the bar, and from the pulpit, errors in grammar, improprieties and vulgarisms which hardly any person of the same class would have fallen into in Great Britain.'

By 1989 the errors, the improprieties and the vulgarisms have become classless and universal. What's more, today's new words don't seem as inspiring as yesterday's. True, we have not yet descended to the level of Newspeak, the language devised by George Orwell for his book *1984*, but we are already in the situation where Alan Siegel, a Miami-based communications and design consultant, is making hundreds of thousands of dollars translating the incomprehensible English of Government departments, banks and insurance companies into English that ordinary people can understand.

And while everyone is *speaking* more, we all seem to be *saying* less. In 1929 C K Ogden and I A Richards devised an English-based language called BASIC (an acronym for British, American, Scientific, International, Commercial) with which they maintained every kind of communication was possible. BASIC used just 850 words, so, understandably, it was attacked from all quarters for the poverty of its vocabulary and for the circumlocution it required for the expression of even the simplest thought – and yet a recent statistical study of telephone speech among modern Americans showed that a vocabulary of only 737 words was used in 96 per cent of all conversations! Shakespeare used 30,000 different words in his plays. James Joyce used 30,000 in *Ulysses*. Today, the man in the street's vocabulary is unlikely to exceed 10,000 words.

The poverty of our day-to-day vocabulary cannot be blamed on the dictionary makers. They only record the words we use. They do not invent them. (The dictionaries that boast that they include no 'racist' words have nothing to boast about. The dictionary maker it not supposed to sit in moral judgement on a word. He is not there to pontificate, but to note the existence of all words and the meanings given to them by their users.) The only people we can blame for what has happened to the language and the use we make of it are ourselves.

The tragedy is that we are the losers. We are not exploiting – not even beginning to exploit – the power of words. You don't need to be a Shakespeare or an Emerson or a Churchill to use words to extraordinary effect. In every aspect of our lives, from business to love (especially love) the person who can use words well has power. For what it's worth, the great seducers have always used words to achieve their ends. So have the great wits. And the great statesmen. And the great confidence tricksters.

T S Eliot felt that words didn't have any innate beauty, that it was their meaning and context that gave them their life. That may be why words like *lullaby* and *marigold* seem to have a special charm and words like *syntax* and *substantival clause* don't. Perhaps the vocabulary of the grammarian only sounds so grim because we loathe grammar so much. '*Ego sum rex Romanus, et supra grammaticam,*' said Sigismund at the Council of Constance in 1414. 'I am king of the Romans, and above grammar.' Today there is hardly an English-speaking person in the word who doesn't feel that he too is above grammar. (I mean 'she' too of course, but I'm afraid the English language hasn't yet produced a satisfactory solution to the 'he or she' dilemma. We're working on it, but for the time being please accept that in the pages that follow when I say he I mean 'he or she' – mostly.)

As you'll discover, from my point of view, good English doesn't necessarily need to be grammatically correct. But it does need to be English that does for you what you want it to do, English that is inventive and fresh and exciting. The more I get to know about words and the more words I get to know the more I enjoy the English language. By the time you get to the end of the book I hope you'll agree.

PART ONE

WORD WORK

Words

Human beings, whether in deepest New Guinea or in darkest Oxfordshire, are distinguishable from other animals by their ability to acquire a system of words and to use it as a means of communication. All known groups of people in the world communicate by speech; all speech systems are infinitely complex though simple enough on the surface; and the majority of the world's population has devised complicated sets of signs to set down speech in written form, these graphic devices being themselves subject to intermittent change, or to substitution, as time goes by.

In 1960, a learned tome called *Language and the Modern World* defined the word *word* as a 'minimum free form consisting of one or more morphemes; [an] arbitrary or

Eye lashes...

conventional segment of utterance.' This, though doubtless accurate, is a somewhat technical definition! It does not take you very far unless you know, for example, what a 'morpheme' is. The definition in the 1976 edition of the *Concise Oxford Dictionary* is more apposite: 'any sound or combination of sounds (or its written or printed symbol, customarily shown with a space on either side of it but none within it) forming [a] meaningful element of speech, conveying an idea or alternative ideas, and capable of serving as a member of, the whole of, or a substitute for, a sentence.' It is important to remember that a word does not necessarily 'stand for' or 'signify' an object: for example, words like *house* or *beehive* do signify objects that can be seen or imagined, but words like *if* and *to* are grammatical words, necessary for the linking together of other words in completed sentences.

A great many words have a base form that cannot be broken down into smaller elements. Take, as an example, the word *father*. It would be useless to analyse it as consisting of *fath−* and *−er* or of *fa−* and *−ther*, as these elements have no meaning now, nor have they had a meaning at any time in the past. If we use the word in its plural form *fathers* we employ the base word *father* and the plural indicator *−s*, and this plural indicator has no formal 'meaning' beyond indicating plurality. The word *fatherly* (eg 'He takes a *fatherly* interest in his younger colleagues') shows the base word modified by an adverbial element *−ly*. In the same way, you can form *fatherhood, fatherless, fatherlike,* and so on, by using other familiar English final elements, *−hood, −less* and *−like*. The same word *father* can be used as a verb (eg 'He *fathered* many children'), in which case it can appear in many forms according to the tense required (*fathers, fathered, fathering,* and with auxiliaries, *will father, will have fathered,* and so on).

What is true of *father* is also true of thousands of words like *man, brother, sister, wife, boy, son, home, house, floor, door, hedge, field,* and so on: all are incapable of analysis into smaller elements however far back we trace their history, and all are capable of forming further words by the affixation of the same kind of additional elements (eg *manly, brotherhood, sisterlike*).

On the other hand some modern words are collapsed forms of what were two words at an earlier stage in English. For example, *lady* comes from the Old English *hlæfdige*, a compound of *hlāf*, and *–dige*, 'a kneader', from a verb meaning 'to knead' related to the word 'dough'; and *lord* comes from the old English *hlāford*, earlier *hlāfweard*, 'loafkeeper'.

These words are a part of our inheritance. Every child born in an English-speaking country finds in due course that it has inherited a fully realized and worked-out language which it needs to master. The same was true in Anglo-Saxon times as far back as records can be traced. In other words Anglo-Saxon – or Old English as some people like to call it – which is recorded from about AD 740 down to the Norman Conquest, was a fully articulated language capable of doing everything required of it. This language, existing in several dialectal forms, was brought to the British Isles in the fifth and sixth centuries AD by warring and migrating tribes known as Angles, Saxons and Jutes, from parts of northern Germany. Members of the same groups who stayed behind in northern Germany, and their kindred in neighbouring areas in what are now Holland and Scandinavia, were soon linguistically distinguishable from those who overran most of Romanized Britain, just as, for example, the English used by people in the British Isles is immediately distinguishable from the English spoken in North America. As time went by, the differences multiplied and now the old dialects of these various peoples in northern Europe have given way to some of the great national languages of Europe – German, Dutch, and the Scandinavian languages, for example, none of them immediately comprehensible to an Englishman. Yet similarities in vocabulary persist. For contemporary evidence of the original close relationship between these languages, look at the German, Dutch and Swedish equivalents of a couple of everyday English words:

English	German	Dutch	Swedish
horn	Horn	hoorn	horn
book	Buch	boek	bok

To reassure yourself that the similarities are not purely co-incidental, compare a slightly longer string of English words, *calf, father, man, milk, mother, son* and *sister*, with the corresponding German words, *Kalb, Vater, Mann, Milch, Mutter, Sohn* and *Schwester*. It would be easy to compile similar lists of English words and their equivalents in Dutch, Danish, Swedish, Icelandic and so on.

So despite the unparalleled growth and development of the English language, elements of continuity remain. One obvious way of tracing this development is to look at the Lord's Prayer in various forms, starting with the Anglo-Saxon version. And if you think you don't know any Anglo-Saxon vocabulary, surprise yourself by reading it out loud:

Anglo Saxon

Faeder ure thu the eart on heofonum
si thin nama gehalgod
to-becume thin rice
gewirthe thin wille on eorthan swa swa on heofenum
urne daeghwaemlice hlaf syle us todaeg
and forgyf us ure gyltas
swa swa we forgyfath urum gyltendum
and ne gelaed thu us on costnunge
ac alys us of yfele, sothlice.

All the words in the Anglo-Saxon version are naturally of native (ie Germanic) origin. You may not have been familiar with most of the words, but I trust you were suitably surprised – and impressed – by the way in which you none the less understood the gist of what was being said.

Wyclif Version (1389)

Oure fadir that art in hevenes
halwid be thi name
thi kyngdom cumme to
be thi wille don as in heven and in erthe
gif to us this day oure breed over other substaunce

and forgeve to us oure dettis
as we forgeve to oure dettours
and leede us nat into temptacioun
but delyvere us fro yvel. Amen

In this much more comprehensible version, the French words *substance, debt, debtors, temptation,* and *deliver,* appear, and the word-order begins to resemble that of the Authorized Version.

Tyndale Version (1525)

O oure father which art in heven
halowed be thy name.
Let thy kyngdom come.
Thy wyll be fulfilled
as well in erth as hit ys in heven.
Geve us this daye oure dayly breade.
And forgeve us oure treaspases
even as we forgeve them whych treaspas us.
Lede us nott in to temptacion
but delyvere us from yvell. Amen.

In this version you'll notice that *substance* has disappeared and that *trespasses* has replaced *debts.*

Authorized Version (1611)

Our father which art in heaven,
hallowed be thy Name.
Thy kingdome come.
Thy will be done,
in earth as it is in heaven.
Give us this day our dayly bread.
And forgive us our debts,
as we forgive our debters.
And leade us not into temptation,
but deliver us from evill:
For thine is the kingdome, and the power,
and the glory, for ever. Amen.

Except for the spelling, and for the use of *debts* and *debtors* this version very closely resembles the one widely used right down to the present day.

Book of Common Prayer (1661)

Our Father which art in heaven,
Hallowed be thy name.
Thy kingdom come.
Thy will be done
in earth as it is in heaven.
Give us this day our daily bread;
And forgive us our trespasses
As we forgive them that trespass against us.
And lead us not into temptation
But deliver us from evil.
For thine is the kingdom, the power,
and the glory. For ever and ever. Amen.

This 1661 version has remained in use in the Church of England and in many of the non-conformist churches ever since. For completeness I had better give the version in the *New English Bible* as well. It is clear even if it isn't particularly poetic.

Our Father in heaven,
thy name be hallowed;
thy kingdom come,
thy will be done,
on earth as in heaven.
Give us today our daily bread.
Forgive us the wrong we have done,
as we have forgiven those who have wronged us.
And do not bring us to the test,
but save us from the evil one.

Finally, and just for fun, here's the Lord's Prayer in Pidgin English. Pidgin, a version of English first developed in the sixteenth century in South America and Africa, is still widely spoken in West Africa and New Guinea.

> Papa belong me-fella, you stop long heaven
> All'e sancru 'im name belong you.
> Kingdom belong you 'e come.
> All 'e hear 'im talk belong you long ground
> all same long heaven.
> Today givem kaikai belong day long me-fella.
> Forgive 'im wrong belong me-fella
> all-same me-fella forgive 'im wrong all
> 'e makem long me-fella.
> You no bring-em me-fella long try 'im.
> Take 'way some t'ing nogood for long me-fella.

These versions of the same prayer represent different points in the long and varied history of the English language. For descriptive purposes it is customary to divide that history into three periods, though the dates chosen as dividing lines are fairly arbitrary, and are a matter of dispute among scholars, since naturally some of the features characteristic of a later period begin to develop in the previous one:

Old English, or Anglo-Saxon, from the earliest written records around 740 to the Norman Conquest.

Middle English, from 1066 to around 1500, when the development of printing introduced a degree of standardization into the written language.

Modern English, from 1500 to the present day.

The language of the sixteenth and seventeenth centuries, taking in the influences of the Renaissance and the great flowering of Elizabethan literature, is sometimes referred to as Early Modern English. Later centuries saw the fixing of the spelling system along with an increase in the influence of prescriptive grammars and, to a lesser extent, dictionaries, which led many to believe that the English language itself had reached a period of stability; later still came the introduction of cheap newspapers, popular education and, in this century, the mass media.

It would take many a weighty volume to describe the development of the English language in scholarly detail, and since I doubt if I could write them and I doubt if you would read them, I'm simply going to attempt to put the essential features of each of the three periods into a nutshell.

Old English

Old English had many inflexions in nouns, adjectives, articles, pronouns and verbs.

Nouns varied inflexion according to number (singular and plural), gender (masculine, feminine, and neuter), case (nominative, accusative, genitive, dative) and declension. Adjectives varied inflexion according to case, gender, number and declension; the rules for using them are quite complicated, but the choice basically depended on whether the adjective was preceded by a definitive article or similar determining word.

The definitive article – there was no indefinite article in Old English: *an* was the numeral 'one' – was also highly inflected. It too varied according to gender (though the plural form is usually the same for all three genders) and number (singular and plural) and, like the adjective, had five cases in the singular (nominative, accusative, genitive, dative and instrumental).

So, for example, 'the good stone', which in Modern English would vary only in the plural, 'the good stones', and then only in the noun, can have the following forms in Old English:

Singular

Nominative	*sē gōd stān*
Accusative	*one gōdne stān*
Dative	*aes gōdes stānes*
Instrumental	*y, on gōde stāne*

Plural

Nominative	*ā gōde stānas*
Accusative	*ā gode stānas*
Genitive	*āra gōdra stāna*
Dative	*āem gōda stānum*

Lazy bone...

The personal pronoun retains a larger number of inflexions than any other part of speech in Modern English. We
still have different persons – *I* (first), *you* (second), *he* (third);
genders – *he* (masculine), *she* (feminine); cases – *I/me,
he/him, she/her*; and numbers – *I/we, he/they*. Old English has
an even greater number of distinctive forms. They exist for
practically all persons, genders and cases, and – one of the
distinctive features of this stage of the language – in addition
to the usual singular and plural there is a dual number for two
people or things, as opposed to three or more. The relevant
forms here are *wit* 'we two', with its inflected forms *uncer*
(genitive) and *unc* (accusative and dative), and *git* 'you two',
with its inflexional variants *incer* and *inc*.

The Old English verb exemplifies the distinctive
Germanic division of verbs into two main classes, the strong
and the weak. Strong verbs indicate tense changes by alteration of their root vowel, as in *sing, sang, sung* and, though
more common in Old than Modern English, they were even
then outnumbered by the weak verbs, which change tense
by the addition of a dental suffix, as in *talk, talked*. In
Modern English verbs of the strong type usually have a different vowel in the present tense (*I sing*), the past tense (*I sang*),
and the past participle (*I have sung*), but Old English
employed more extensive variation. The 'principal parts' of
Old English strong verbs are usually represented by the infin-
itive (*drīfan* 'to drive'), the first and third person past tense
singular (*ic drāf* 'I drove'), the plural past tense (*we drīfon*
'we drove'), and the past participle (*ic haebbe drīfen*
(or *gedrifen*) 'I have driven'). *Drīfan* is a member of the first
class of strong verbs. There are seven general classes in
Old English, all of which have a regular sequence of vowel
changes in the root.

In addition to this variation according to class, Old
English verbs had three moods, indicative, subjunctive, and
imperative, and the usual two numbers and three persons.
The subjunctive mood was used much more commonly than
it is in Modern English, as were impersonal constructions.
Many verbs (and also nouns) began with the perfective
prefix *ge−* (shown in the alternative past participle form
gedrifen given above) which indicated the completion of an

action, eg *climban* 'to climb', but *geclimban* 'to climb and reach the top'.

During the Old English period almost the whole of the vocabulary was of native origin. Many of the words were very simple ones that have survived with little alteration to modern times:

Old English	Modern English
clyppan	to clip
frēond	friend
gōd	good
hand, hond	hand
nēd	need
rēad	red
scip	ship
springan	to spring
swēte	sweet
wegan	to weigh

But many common Old English words died out later and were either replaced by other native words or by Latin, French, and other alien words, or developed more specialized meanings: OE *milts* 'mercy' later replaced by *mercy* (French *merci*, from Latin *mercēs*, *mercēdem*). *Milts* is not recorded after the fourteenth century. OE *sine* 'treasure' was replaced by *treasure* (from Old French). OE *steorfan* 'to diet' was replaced in most uses by *die* (Old Norse *deyja*), but survives as *starve* 'to die of hunger'. OE *weorpan* 'the throw' was replaced in most uses by *throw* (OE *thrāwan*) or *case* (Old Norse *kasta*), but survives as *warp* 'seasoned timber does not warp').

The principal exceptions to the Germanic origin of words in Old English are a few religious terms from Latin, for example, *apostle, cell, cloister, demon, idol, prophet* and *sabbath*, most of which were naturally adopted during the process of the Christianizing of Britain. The earlier Roman occupation left very little impression on the English language, save in place names. One of the best known and most widespread place-name elements is of Latin origin. Latin *castra* 'camp', in the forms −*caster,* −*cester* and −*chester*, appears in such names as Lancaster, Doncaster, Gloucester, Worcester, Winchester, Dorchester and, of course, Chester itself.

The absence of Latin influence from the period of Roman occupation is not really surprising, as the Anglo-Saxon invaders arrived after the departure of most of the representatives of the Roman empire, but the paucity of vocabulary of Celtic origin in Old English is a matter for pause. The encounter between the Anglo-Saxons and the Celtic-speaking peoples who had arrived at an earlier date was a classic example of the confrontation of two peoples sharing the same land and, in due course, the same religion (Christianity), but speaking entirely different languages. The politically dominant Anglo-Saxons found little reason to adopt the culture, and hence the language, of the submerged Celts, many of whom in fact fled to the west, and a mere handful of words made their way from the Celtic languages into Old English. One of the few popular words is *brocc* 'badger'. Place names, however, frequently contain Celtic elements, such as *torr* 'high rock' and *cumb* 'valley', and various river and hill names are of Celtic origin, including the *Thames.*

Towards the end of the Old English period the Scandinavian invasions, resulting in the eventual conquest of a large part of England, introduced many Scandinavian loan words, but the new inhabitants spoke a closely related language and so to the end of the Old English period the predominantly Germanic character of English remained undisturbed.

Middle English

During the Middle-English period words poured into the language from French. Many were connected with the church and Christian beliefs and practices. The *Oxford English Dictionary* records in the twelfth century such words as *cardinal, chaplain, sacrament* and *sermon*; in the thirteenth century large numbers, including *abbess, abbey, baptism, clergy, crucifix, damnation, devout, friar, heresy, hermit, incense, ordain, penance, prayer, prelate, saviour, surplice, temptation* and *trinity*; and in the fourteenth century *communion, confession, dean, divine, lectern, redemption, sanctity, sanctuary* and many others. Similarly, many of our legal words came into English during the Middle-English period, as well as many used in law but also with a wider application. In the twelfth century are recorded, for example, *justice* and *prison*; in the thirteenth, *acquit, assault, assize, condemn, evidence, felon, gaol, hue and cry, inquest, judgement, libel, pardon, pillory, plaintiff, seisin, slander, suit, summons, trespass* and *verdict*; in the fourteenth, *advocate, arrest, attorney, convict, crime, defendant, entail, equity, fraud, indict, indictment, juror, legacy, perjury, petition* and *tort*; in the fifteenth, *jurist, larceny* and *punishment*.

For many centuries French was the language of government and administration, as well as of law, and it is not surprising to find the introduction of many words of French origin connected with public affairs and the organization of society. The twelfth century sees the first record of *baron, council, countess* and *duke*; the thirteenth, *alliance, authority, bailiff, chamberlain, constable, court, courtier, demesne, empire, exchequer, govern, governor, homage, majesty, manor, mayor, marshal, minister, parliament, peer, prince, realm, rebel, reign, sceptre, servant, slave, sovereign, squire, statute, traitor, treason, tyrant* and *warden*; the fourteenth, *administer, assembly, castellan, councillor, duchess, governance, marquis, retinue, royal, subsidy, tax, treaty, tyranny* and *viscount*; the fifteenth, *baroness, peasant* and *revenue*.

Since the upper classes were for a long time French speaking the vocabulary of fashion, food, and social life generally, also became permeated with words of French origin. It is well known that the names of various meats as articles of diet derive from French: *beef, mutton, pork* and *venison* all appear towards the end of the thirteenth century, and the *Oxford English Dictionary* records *veal* first in *The Merchant's Tale* by the fourteenth-century poet, Geoffrey Chaucer. The names of cooking processes frequently entered the language from French during this period – *boil, fry,* mince, stew and *roast* are examples. The opening up of trade with the east brought the names of numerous spices and condiments into English through French – *spice* itself is a Middle-English borrowing – and exotic fruits such as *dates, oranges, lemons, pomegranates* and *peaches* made their way on to the English table. The English began to wear *coats, cloaks, collars, robes* and *veils* during the thirteenth century; *boots, buckles, buttons, frocks, galoshes, garters, gowns* and *mittens* during the fourteenth; and *trains* during the fifteenth.

Thanks to an outstanding English teacher (Harold Gardiner by name, a great man), I became a fan of the works of Chaucer (1340?–1400) at the age of fourteen and marvelled then, as I do now, at how easily comprehensible his Middle English is to speakers of Modern English. At school we read him out loud, a technique I recommend to anyone who finds the prospect of reading Chaucer somewhat daunting. Here, for example, is the famous description of the Knight in the *Prologue* to the *Canterbury Tales* (showing the words of French origin in italics):

A Knight ther was, and that a worthy man,
That fro the tyme that he first bigan
To ryden out, he loved *chivalrye*,
Trouthe and *honour*, fredom and *curteisye*.
Ful worthy was he in his lordes *werre*,
And thereto hadde he riden (no man ferre)
As wel in Cristendom as hethenesse,
And ever *honoured* for his worthinesse.
At Alisaundre he was, whan it was wonne;
Ful ofte tyme he hadde the bord bigonne
Aboven alle *naciouns* in Pruce . . .
And evermore he hadde a *sovereyn prys*.
And though that he were worthy, he was wys,
And if his *port* as meke as is a mayde
He never yet no *vileinye* ne sayde
In al his lyf, unto no maner wight.
He was a *verray parfit gentil* knight.

English grammar also changed radically during the Middle English period, owing in particular to the loss or reduction of the Old-English inflexional system described earlier. Idiomatic uses of prepositions increased enormously to convey those relationships which had previously been indicated by case endings. The subjunctive mood generally became indistinguishable from the indicative. The verb phrase also became more complex, with greater freedom in the use of auxiliaries. The verbal system was also modified by the loss of many strong verbs and the transfer of large numbers of others to the weak pattern.

In the personal pronouns many of the Old-English distinctions were retained, as they are today, though the dual forms were lost completely and do not appear after the thirteenth century. The dative and accusative cases merged, the accusative (*hit*) being chosen for the neuter, and the datives *him* and *her* in the masculine and feminine. The dative form also survived in the plural. *His* as a neuter genitive was replaced by *(h)it* (*its* being a later development). The most interesting innovations were *they, their* and *them* as plural forms and *she* as a feminine singular. The *th*— forms were adopted from Scandinavian, and began to replace the native *h*— forms first in areas of strong Scandinavian influence. The reflexes of the Old English forms *hi (he), here (their)* and *hem (them)*, remained in use throughout the period, especially in the south. The nominative *they* first became general – Chaucer's usual inflexions are *thei, here, hem* – and later *their* and *them* also became the normal English plurals. Unlike *they, their* and *them*, whose origins are clear, *she* is still a mystery. Though a number of scholars have put forward theories concerning its origin, none has been universally accepted. The Old-English feminine nominative singular was *heo*, and the new form clearly gained in popularity because of its distinctness from the masculine forms.

Modern English

Except in pronunciation most of the main features of present-day English can be discerned as early as 1500, but at that date the frequency and distribution of many familiar features was quite different.

Spelling gradually began to become fixed after the introduction of printing in the last quarter of the fifteenth century, though it did not settle down into its present form until about 1800. This process of normalization was helped by the appearance of standard English dictionaries, the first of which was Robert Cawdry's *A Table Alphabeticall* (1604), and the regularization of spelling was further assisted by the proponents of 'correctness' in the eighteenth century, the Augustan Age, notably Dr Samuel Johnson and Jonathan Swift.

The American way of spelling words departed radically from our own as far back as the beginning of the nineteenth century, chiefly through the influence of Noah Webster's *American Dictionary of the English Language* (1828), and the two greatest varieties of English are separated by such well-known differences as:

British	American
colour	color
travelled	traveled
aesthetic	esthetic
centre	center
analyse	analyze

Word order has become even more fixed than in Middle English. For example, the sentence 'the dog bit the boy' cannot be expressed in any other way (eg 'the boy bit the dog', 'the dog the boy bit', 'dog the bit boy the') without reversing the meaning or producing a nonsensical sentence. That is not to say that in Modern English we must *always* place sentences in the same strict order. Disturbance of normal word order is common in poetry, for example:

Much have I travell'd in the realms of gold,
And many goodly states and kingdoms seen;

However, in normal contexts and unless you happen to be John Keats the rules governing the positioning of elements of the sentence are now quite rigid.

The main additions to the vocabulary during the early Modern English period are learned words from Latin and Greek, frequently called 'inkhorn terms' because of their bookish character. Some were introduced in a conscious effort to increase the resources of the English language; others originated in affectation. Many proved superfluous and have since fallen into disuse.

Innumerable words that we would find it hard to imagine being without are first recorded during the sixteenth and seventeenth centuries. Here is a random sample, with the language of origin and first recorded date (according to the *Oxford English Dictionary*):

Bow Legs...

abdomen (Latin) 1541
anonymous (Greek) 1601
apparatus (Latin) 1628
atmosphere (Greek through Latin) 1638
botanic (Greek through Latin) 1656
catastrophe (Greek) 1579
complication (Latin) 1611
defect, *vb* (Latin) 1579
encyclopaedia (pseudo-Greek from Latin) 1531
excursion (Latin) 1579
fabulous (Latin) 1546
fluctuate (Latin) 1634
frugal (Latin) 1598
gesticulate (Latin) 1601
humiliate (Latin) 1533–34
infirmary (Latin) 1625
meditate (Latin) *c* 1580
nodule (Latin) 1600
obscene (Latin) 1593
parsimonious (Latin) 1598
pendulum (Latin) 1660
pollen (Latin) 1523
polygamist (Greek) 1637
radiate (Latin) 1649
ritual (Latin) 1570
scheme (Greek through Latin) 1553
species (Latin) 1551
syndrome (Greek through Latin) 1541
tautology (Greek through Latin) 1579
thermometer (Greek) 1633
torpedo (Latin) *c* 1520
typical (Latin) 1598
vacuum (Latin) 1599
vitreous (Latin) 1646
zoology (Latin and Greek) 1669

During the nineteenth and twentieth centuries the English language has continued to be hospitable to foreign words. The rise of literature in English in South Africa,

Australia, New Zealand, and elsewhere, has meant the introduction into print of numerous terms from Afrikaans, aboriginal languages, Maori, and so on. Native terms were frequently adopted for flora and fauna in particular. The blossoming of all the sciences has kept the classical languages alive as formative elements in English, and the international nature of the scientific community facilitates the adoption of technical terms from other European and non-European languages. America has seen the assimilation of countless terms from the languages of its many immigrants, Yiddish, Norwegian, German and the rest, and from its Spanish-speaking neighbours in the south.

The sheer variety of words which can be met in works written in English can be illustrated from the new vocabulary beginning with the letter 'c' recorded in the *Supplement to the Oxford English Dictionary*. The degree of naturalization of these words varies considerably. The foreign origin of some is on the way to being forgotten; others will never be used except when describing foreign countries and their customs. But all are a testimony to the vitality of the English language and the enterprise of its speakers.

Latin is represented there in its classical medieval, and modern forms. In the sciences classical Latin has given us, for example, *candela*, a unit of luminosity first recorded in 1950; in botany and zoology *calamistrum* (in the original language a curling iron), a comb-like structure found on the legs of certain spiders, first recorded in 1866; *calcicole* 'that grows best in calcareous soil', 1882; *cauliflory*, the production of flowers directly from the trunk or branches, 1903. Modern Latin furnishes the terms for many medical conditions, such as *carcinomatosis* (1905), *catathymia* (a psychiatric term, 1934), *causalgia* (1872), *cervicitis* (1889), and *claustrophobia* (1879). It is particularly a source of botanical and zoological terms, such as:

    cameloid, 1885
    canid, 1889
    catasetum (a plant), 1829
    catastomid (a fish), 1889
    cattlyeye (a plant), 1828

cecropia (a tree), 1833 and
cecropia (a moth), 1868
celosia (a plant), 1807
cephalodiscus, 1882
ceratosaurus (an extinct reptile), 1884

In non-scientific contexts Latin has also given us, for example, *campus*, now a common word for the grounds of a college or university, *cancellandum*, a printing term (1923), *cantharus* (1842), *cappa*, a cope (1859), the phrase *carpe diem* enjoining us to make the most of the present time (Lord Byron in 1817), *castrum*, a Roman encampment (1836), and *casus belli*, an act regarded as justifying war (J S Mill in 1849). The medieval form of the language is represented by *canterist*, a chantry priest (1800), *centaurea*, a plant (1829), and *conductus*, a class of musical composition (1801). Latin elements also combine freely with English or other long-established formative elements to produce such words as *cacuminal* in phonetics (1862), *callosal* in anatomy (1868), *caloric* (1865), *campimeter* (1889), *caritive* in grammar (1860), *castrative* (1943), *cellifugal* (1900) and *cementoma*, a form of tumour on the teeth (1893).

Greek, the other great classical language, is also most in evidence in words beginning with the latter 'c' in medical, psychological and other scientific fields. Examples include *cataclinal*, a rare geological term (1875), *cataphoresis*, a medical word (1889), *cathectic* in psychology (1927), *cathexis* (1922), *chaetigerous* in zoology (1896), *chaetotaxy* (1893), *chalone*, the biochemical opposite of 'hormone' (1914), and the medical *chiropractic* (1898). There are also a number of religious and theological words, such as *cataphatic*, an adjective meaning 'defining God positively, or by positive statements' (1869), *cathisma*, a portion of the psalter in the Greek church (1850), and *chartophylax*, an officer in the household of the Patriarch of Constantinople (1879). Among the other miscellaneous words of Greek origin are *catalexis*, a term in prosody, and *chalcenterous* 'with bowels of bronze', that is, 'tough' (1946)! A further testimony to the vitality of the classical languages in English word formation is the continued creation of words of mixed Latin and Greek derivation. Such are, for example, *calciphilous* (1909) and *calciphobus* (1907), botanical terms for suited or not suited to chalky soil, and *camerostome* (1888), a zoological term formed from modern Latin and Greek elements.

By far the greatest number of modern foreign loans in the letter 'c' derive from French. As in the Middle-English period, French leads the field in cuisine and fashion, themselves both words of French origin. During the last two centuries the English have become acquainted with the taste of *canapés* (1890), *cassis*, a blackcurrant liqueur (1907), *cassoulet* (1940), *charcuterie* (1858), *chaud froid*, cooked meat, fish etc served cold in aspic jelly or sauce (1892), *chiffonnade* (1877), *chipolatas*, which the French themselves adopted from the Italian (1877), *choucroute* (1849), *coq au vin* (*c.* 1938), *courgettes* (1931), *couverture*, chocolate suitable for covering cakes, etc (1935), *crépinette* (1877), *croustades* (1845), *croûtes* (1906), and *croûtons* (1806). They learned that you could serve coffee from a *cafetière* (1846) and buy pork from a *charcutier* (1894), and wine lovers became acquainted with the terms *casse*, incipient souring of certain wines (1883), *cru* (1824), and *cuvée* (1833).

From the world's fashion centre came the new materials *charmante* (1922), *charmelaine* (1923), *charmeuse* (1907), *cloqué* (1950), *crêpeline* (1873) and *crin* (1875), which could appear in the colours *ciel* (1910) or *crevette* (1884). English women could consider whether to wear a *cache peigne* on their hats (1873), the *canezou* (1827), a blouse-like garment which was temporarily in fashion in the nineteenth century, or a *casaquin* (1879), and first men (1842) and then more commonly women (1911) took to *culottes*. All could take their problems concerning *couture* (1908) to a *couturier* (1899) or his female counterpart the *couturière* (1818); women's hair could be styled by a *coiffeuse* (1870); and those really interested in the art and practice of beauty culture could study *cosmetology* (1855). Evenings could be spent playing *chemin de fer* (1891), and the conversation could be spiced with French phrases such as *capable de tout* (1899), *cherchez la femme!* (1893), the *crème de la crème* (1848), and *cri de coeur* (1905).

The French contribution to the arts is recognized in the adoption of numerous items of vocabulary. In ballet and the dance we find *cambré* (1913), *chainé* (1946), *changement de pieds* (1840), *chassé croisé* (1883), and *ciseaux* (1892). Words in other artistic fields include *champlevé* in enamel work (1856), *chansonnier* (1887), *chanteuse* (1888), *chef d'orchestre* (1855), *cinéaste*, a cinema enthusiast (1926), the more recent *cinema vérité* (1963), *ciré perdue*, a method of casting bronze by making a model with a wax surface, enclosing it in a mould, melting the wax out, and running in the metal between the core and the mould (1876), *collage*, now practised by many a British primary-school pupil (1919), *conte*, a short story (1891), *couac*, a marvellous onomatopoeic word for the sound produced by bad blowing on the clarinet, oboe, or bassoon (1876), *craquelure* (1914), *criblé* (1879), *cuivré*, a musical direction meaning 'brassy' (1931), and, less to the credit of the French, *cabotin*, a low-class actor (1903), which gives us *cabotinism* (1926) and *cabotinage* (1894), 'the life or behaviour characteristic of low-class actors', with, according to the *Supplement to the Oxford English Dictionary*, 'implications of "playing to the gallery"'.

Of the numerous French loans beginning with 'c' which do not yield so easily to classification, by far the best known are *camouflage*, recorded in English both as a noun and as a verb in 1917, the indispensable *carton* (1906), though used to designate the cardboard box from which such boxes are made in 1891, and *chauffeur*, first used for an automobilist (1899), a sense now obsolete, then with its usual sense in 1902.

The contribution of German as represented in the letter 'c' is virtually confined to scientific terminology, though this would by no means be true of every letter of the alphabet. We find, for example:

cardol (1848)
carvacrol (1854)
celloidin (1883)
chemiluminescence (1905)
chimyl alcohol (1924)

In philosophy and linguistics is *categorical* (1912). It is notable that the German words from which these are derived are almost all formed on Latin and Greek elements, as is much native British scientific terminology. Native (Germanic) German words can be found entering English in other parts of the alphabet.

Among the other modern European languages, Italian influences English most in the areas of music and cookery. Musical terms include, for example, *cabaletta*, an aria or part of an aria (1842), *cantino*, the treble string of a violin or similar instrument (1876), *capo tasto*, a device for raising the pitch of a stringed instrument (1876), *cembalo* a harpsichord (1865), and the direction *con sordino* 'with the mute or damper' (1825). Foodstuffs introduced from Italian include *calabrese*, a variety of broccoli (1930), *canelloni*, known in its modern form since 1937 but appearing as *cannelons* from 1845, and *cassata* (1927). The English-speaking peoples have also begun to drink *cappuccino*, espresso coffee with milk, first recorded in 1948.

Of the remaining Italian loans the most familiar is *confetti* (1815), which in Italy was bon bons, plaster, or paper imitations of these thrown during carnival, and which in English has now replaced the rice traditionally thrown on a bride. If you're familiar with *confetti* I trust you'll be less at home with *Cosa Nostra*, a name for the Mafia in the United States (1963). Other, innocuous, words include the term of endearment *carissima* (1957), *cassone*, a large coffer (1882), *ceppo*, the cemented glacial gravels found in northern Italy (1881), *contrapposto*, a term used in the visual arts (1903), and *credenza*, a sideboard (1880).

The influence of Spanish on English vocabulary in the nineteenth and twentieth centuries is complicated by the separate development of the Spanish language in the Americas. Many loan words represent distinctive American-Spanish forms which have become familiar in Britain through the English of the United States, though the terminology of bullfighting, for example, is very much of European origin. In the letter 'c' are found *capeador* (1909), *cogida* (1923), *cornada* (1932), and *corrida* (1898). Spanish has also given us *calandria*, a closed cylindrical vessel used, among other

Palmtree...

things, in some nuclear reactors (1929), the card game *canasta*, which is of Uruguayan origin (1948), the interjection *caramba!* (1835), and *caudillo*, best known as the title assumed by General Franco (1852). In America, the ebullient Spanish-speaking Latin Americans have introduced us to a number of rumbustious dances, including the *cha-cha- (-cha)* (1954) and the *conga* (1935). From American Spanish we also derived the – perhaps more essential – *cafeteria* (1839) and the *cantina* (1892).

The closely related Portuguese language is represented by a smaller number of disparate terms, mostly relating to Brazil and other Portuguese-speaking South American countries. Examples include *Caboclo*, used chiefly for a civilized Amerindian descended from Brazilian aboriginals (1816), *candiru*, ultimately from Tupi, a kind of blood-sucking catfish (1841), and *carbonado*, a variety of diamond found in Brazil (1853).

The nineteenth century saw some of the first extensive descriptions of Jewish life and social and religious customs. We therefore find the earliest English record of Hebrew words such as *Chagigah*, the voluntary sacrifices offered at Passover, *Pentecost*, and *Tabernacles* (1846), *Chanuk(k)ah*, a Jewish festival (1891), *charoset(h)* (1885), *chedar*, a Hebrew school (1882), *cherem*, excommunication by the Synagogue (1829), and *chuppah*, a canopy under which marriages are performed (1876).

Hebrew was formerly restricted to religious contexts. The more light-hearted side of Jewish life and character is reflected in languages such as Yiddish, which has given so many expressive colloquialisms to American English. There are few in 'c' – Yiddish is represented only by *caser*, a slang term for a crown or, in the United States, a dollar (1849), *chutzpah*, 'brazen impudence, gall' (1892), and *cocum*, used of something lucky or, alternatively, correct (1839) – but they give a taste of the Yiddish contribution to the richness of English.

As I mentioned earlier the Celtic languages left little impression on early English so it is particularly gratifying to see a number of Irish, Welsh, Scottish-Gaelic, and even Manx words, of however limited occurrence and distribution, making an appearance in English in the last two centuries. The *ceilidh* (Irish *céilidhe*, Scottish-Gaelic *cēilidh*) has been popularized in recent years, but is first recorded in 1875, and few can have failed to become acquainted with the *corgi* (Welsh, from *corr*, a dwarf, and *ci*, a dog), although the name is first recorded only in 1926 (appropriately enough, the year of the birth of Her Majesty the Queen). Other words are of more restricted use: *caman*, from Gaelic, the stick used in the game of shinty (1891), *carval*, a Manx name for a carol (1873), *cleit*, a local name from Gaelic for a small shelter (1825), *cluricaune*, an elf in Irish mythology (1825), *crubeen*, an Anglo-Irish name for an animal's foot (1847) and *cwm*, a Welsh word for a valley which has become more widely used in physical geography.

Much further away from home than the Celtic fringe, English-speaking people confronted the many languages of India. The period of British colonization and empire has left us with one indispensable item of vocabulary, the adjective *cushy*, an Anglo-Indian word deriving from Hindustani and first recorded in 1915. Another loan from the same language is *chukka*, the name of the periods into which a game of polo is divided (1898). With these two exceptions, Hindustani words beginning with 'c' apply only to Indian concepts and institutions, but if you take the rest of the alphabet you will find there are scores of everyday English words that have joined the language from the Indian sub-Continent.

Many other languages are mentioned in the etymologies of words beginning with 'c' in the *Supplement to the Oxford English Dictionary* including, in alphabetical order:

Afrikaans	*chokka*, a squid (1902)
Burmese	*chaung*, a watercourse (1945)
	Chindit, a member of the Allied Forces fighting behind the Japanese lines in Burma during World War II (1943)
Carib	*cassiri*, a liquor (1796)
Chinese	*campoi*, a kind of tea (1842)
	cheongsam, a woman's garment (1957)
	chop suey (1888)
	chow mein (1903)
Fante	*cedi*, the basic monetary unit of Ghana (1965)
Hungarian	*csardas*, a dance (1860)
Norwegian	*cataclastic*, a geological term proposed by a Norwegian in 1885 (1887)
Russian	*chernozem*, a geological term (1842)
	chervonetz, a Soviet bank note (1923)
Serbian	*chetnik*, a Balkan guerrilla (1909)
Telugu	*kattimandoo*, the name of a gum and also the plant from which it is obtained (1851)
Tibetan	*chang*, a drink (1800)
Tupi	*caatinga*, a type of forest in Brazil (1846)
Turkish	*choga*, an Afghan garment with long sleeves (1869)
Vietnamese	*Caodaism*, the name of a religion, from words meaning 'great palace' plus the regular English suffix '−ism' (1937)

So many of the words mentioned entered the language during the nineteenth century that they could give a misleading impression of the amount of innovation during the twentieth century. In fact, the number of new words coming into the language this century is vast. Let me list just a few of the words and phrases, of various origins, which were first recorded in print in the years from 1929 to 1970. Some were deliberate – but the great majority made their way into print quite casually in the *Reader's Digest, Time* magazine, or other periodicals, and may well have been in use orally at a slightly earlier date:

   1929 astronautics
   1930 axel (skating)
   1931 microwave
   1932 malnourishment
   1933 abseil
   1934 Agit-prop
   1935 autition (vb)
   1936 Maginot Line
   1937 autobahn
   1938 Moral Rearmament
   1939 ack-ack
   1940 Mae West (life-jacket)
   1941 majorette
   1942 astronavigation
   1943 acronym
   1944 aerosol
   1945 microsleep
   1946 microdot
   1947 apartheid
   1948 automation
   1949 male menopause
   1950 aqualung
   1951 Maoism
   1952 to take the mickey out of (someone)
   1953 adventure playground
   1954 non-U (A S C Ross)
   1955 admass (J B Priestley and J Hawkes)

1956 brinkmanship (Adlai Stevenson)
1957 Angry Young Man (G Fearon)
1958 aerospace (W A Heflin)
1959 microbus
1960 biorhythm
1961 mini (abbreviation of mini-car, mini-cab)
1962 non-event (I Gilmore)
1963 Mandrax
1964 monokini
1965 metrication (E McIntosh)
1966 Nibmar ('no independence before majority African rule')
1967 monohull
1968 nuffieldite (name of mineral)
1969 misregister (vb)
1970 biofeedback (Dr Barbara Brown)

In the age of Thatcherism and post-Reagonomics, when the occupant of the Vatican travels by Popemobile and the occupants of Buckingham Palace frequently 'go walkabout', whether we are yuppies (or wrinklies or even crumblies) we all know that new words are finding their way into the language almost daily. There is nothing new about this. For centuries, in terms of richness and diversity, there has been no language to rival English.

Wonder Words

Among the hundreds of thousands of words in the English language some are long, some are short, some are familiar and formed on common roots and affixes, some are exotic with extraordinary consonant and vowel combinations.
The longest word in the *Oxford English Dictionary* is:

floccinaucinihilipilification

which has 29 letters. It is made up of a number of Latin words all signifying 'at a small price' or 'at nothing' and the English suffix *−fication*, and is a humorous word for 'the action or habit of estimating as worthless'. It is first recorded in 1741 in a letter by the poet William Shenstone, and was later used by Robert Southey and Sir Walter Scott. However, longer words have been attested since the main part of the *Oxford English Dictionary* was completed. The *Guinness Book of Records* notes a chemical, tryptophan synthetase A protein, with the formula $C_{1289}H_{2051}N_{343}O_{375}S_8$ and a name consisting of 1,913 letters! Webster's *Third International Dictionary*, published in 1961, includes a 45-letter name for a lung disease found among miners:

pneumonoultramicroscopicsilicovolcanoconiosis

A word often considered to be the longest regularly formed on English affixes is *antidisestablishmentarianism*, with 28 letters, though no one seems to have found a context in which it is generally useful, except in illustrations of how long a word can be built up in this way. There is, however, a 37-letter adverb:

praetertranssubstantiationalistically

in the novel *Untimely Ripped* by Mark McShane, published in 1963.

Of course you can invent any number of long nonsense words. Perhaps the best known in recent years is:

supercalifragilisticexpialidocious

with 34 letters. There is scope for length in the invention of echoic words too. Let me end this enumeration of some of the monsters of English with the sound of a fall in the third paragraph of James Joyce's novel *Finnegans Wake* (1939) – a pretty long fall requiring 100 letters:

bababadalgharaghtakamminarronnkonnbronntonnerronn-
tuonnthunntrovarrhounawnskawntoohoohoordenenthur-
nuk!

The shortest words in English are much easier to think of – the vowel symbols *a, i, o,* and *u* (rarely *e*) all occur as independent words. However, the variety of uses to which they have been put may surprise you. For *a* the use as the indefinite article, as in 'a book', inevitably leads the list. This is its only function in modern standard English. In representations of Scottish speech it is also used for 'all', though here it's usually followed by an apostrophe *a'*. In the past *a* has appeared for the pronouns 'he' (this use is found in Shakespeare, but did not survive the seventeeth century), 'she', and 'they' (in the thirteenth and fourteenth centuries); right into the nineteenth century it represented a worn-down form of 'have', still used in some informal and dialectal speech but now usually spelt 'ha' even though the 'h' may not be pronounced; it was used for reduced forms of the prepositions 'in', 'on', and 'of', and for a small number of other obsolete prepositions and conjunctions; exclamations of surprise, admiration, or grief, now usually 'ah', were also occasionally spelt *a* in Middle English; this interjection was also used prefixed to a proper name as a war cry, as in 'A Gordon!' (in Sir Walter Scott's poem *Marmion*), but modern writers tend to treat it as though it were the indefinite article.

I is, of course, the first person singular pronoun; it is also used as a shortened form of the preposition 'in', though usually with an apostrophe, in such archaic oaths as 'i' faith'.

O is now most commonly an interjection ('O dear!' 'O for a drink!'); it is sometimes used as a shortened form of 'of', the best known instance being 'o'clock'; in Middle English it was used in some parts of the country for the numeral 'one', and also with the meaning 'always, ever'. A verb 'o', meaning 'to decorate with small circular discs' is also recorded once in the seventeenth century in its past participle 'oed'.

U once appeared as a variant of 'yew', but this is now obsolete; in recent years it has become common, especially in

Blank stare

advertising copy, as a spelling of the second person pronoun
'you'.

Consonantal symbols can only appear by themselves as
abbreviations. A great exploiter of the use of the initial letter
in place of the complete word was P G Wodehouse, one of the
twentieth century's most delightful – and prolific – novelists.
The most characteristic example is 'eggs and b' for 'eggs and
bacon', but there are many more. For example, in *Jeeves in
the Offing*, first published in 1960, you'll find:

> h.w.b. (hot water bottle)
> a hollow g. (groan)
> f.b. (fevered brow)
> to cut a long story s. (short)
> out of the q. (question)
> nervous s. (strain)
> see at a g. (glance)
> break the n. (news)
> up to me to do the s.t. (same thing) by him
> the coast seemed c. (clear)
> picking my words with c. (care)
> I could hardly b. my e. (believe my ears)
> no exception to the r. (rule)

Wodehouse also used shortened forms of many other words,
for example:

> the inev. (inevitable)
> occ. (occasion)
> posish. (position)
> situash. (situation)
> subj. (subject)

Wodehouse's vocabulary is highly individual and entertaining. He seldom coined words, though he is occasionally the
first written source cited by the *Supplement to the Oxford
English Dictionary* – for 'gruntled', for example. He had,
however, a very sensitive ear for the latest slang, and was
often among the earliest recorders of a new vogue expression.
One of his great specialities was euphemism, or the sub-

stitution of a circumlocution for a well-known object, as in 'gasper' for 'cigarette'. He also commonly converted words and phrases into different parts of speech, for instance 'French cheffing' (what Bertie Wooster's aunt's French chef does) and 'upping with the lark' (from the phrase 'to get up with the lark'). And he had a marvellous array of expressions for people in general and characters in particular.

Here are some typical Wodehouse words and phrases, with occasional explanations and comments for those on which definite information is available:

to beetle around, 'beetle' meaning to fly off, make one's way, etc, is first recorded by the *Supplement to the OED* in 1919; Wodehouse was using it in 1923.

beezer, the nose. In the *OED Supplement* from 1915; being used by Wodehouse in the 30s.

billiken, 'a small, squat, smiling figure used as a mascot'. The first known use is in a Wodehouse novel (1914).

bimbo, a contemptuous name for a person. First recorded in 1919; in a Wodehouse novel in 1924.

blister, a derogatory name for an annoying person, dating from at least 1806.

bish, a jocular abbreviation of 'bishop' used as a noun and as a verb. The *OED Supplement* records it first in 1875.

to bite the ears off, to borrow from. 'Bite' meaning to cadge or borrow from is also Australian slang.

buttle, to do a butler's work. In the *OED Supplement* from 1918.

crumb, an objectionable person. First recorded in 1918; used by Wodehouse in 1930.

crumpet, person; usually in 'old crumpet', a term of endearment. 'Crumpet' is first recorded in 1900; 'old crumpet' in 1920, then in Wodehouse in 1923.

crust, impudence, effrontery. Wodehouse has the first known literary use in 1923, but it appears in a glossary of American dialect terms in 1900.

to have a dash (at), to make an attempt. The first known use is in a Wodehouse novel in 1923.

came the dawn, a cliché announcing daybreak, first appearing in 1927 in Wodehouse's *Meet Mr Mulliner*.

to hand (or pass) in one's dinner-pail, to die. The first known examples date from 1905; Wodehouse uses it in 1922.

dirty work at the crossroads, a phrase recorded first in 1914 in a Wodehouse novel.

to put on dog, to put on pretentious airs. This was not a new expression when Wodehouse used it; it is first recorded in 1871.

down to earth, back to reality. The first known example is in *Very Good, Jeeves* in 1930.

elbow, in 'to give someone the elbow' (to dismiss).

even-Stephen, a rhyming intensified form of 'even', first recorded in 1866.

up to the eyebrows, an exaggeration of 'up to the eyes'. The first known example is in *Carry On, Jeeves!* in 1925.

face, as a slang term of address this is first known from Wodehouse (1923).

flesh and blood, 'old flesh and blood', sometimes 'old flesh and b.' is one of Bertie Wooster's ways of addressing or referring to his aunt.

foggy between the ears, not very intelligent or perceptive.

fungus, a beard. The first recorded example is in Wodehouse's *Sam the Sudden* (1925).

galley-slave stuff, rowing.

gaper, an easy catch in cricket. First used in 1903, by Wodehouse.

Gawd-help-us (or *Gawdelpus*), a helpless or exasperating person. Used by Wodehouse in 1931, but first recorded in 1912.

gimme, as a noun meaning 'acquisitiveness' or 'greed'. First recorded in *Meet Mr Mulliner* (1927).

goop, a stupid or fatuous person. Others used this well before Wodehouse.

gosh-awfulness, first recorded in *Right Ho, Jeeves* (1934).

gruntled, pleased, satisfied. The first known example of this back-formation from 'disgruntled' is in *The Code of the Woosters* (1938).

half-portion, a small or insignificant person. First recorded in 1919, in a Wodehouse novel.

down the hatch, down the throat. As a toasting or drinking phrase this is known from 1931.

to haul up one's slacks, to speak angrily.

hornswoggle, to cheat or hoodwink. This is used from the beginning of the nineteenth century.

johnny, a person.

kick, a pocket; in 'in one's kick', in one's possession. This word is first recorded in 1851.

lame-brain, a stupid person. First used in *Mr Mulliner Speaking* (1929)

loony-bin, a mental hospital. First recorded in *My Man Jeeves* (1919).

lulu, a remarkable person or thing. This expression, originally American, was first recorded in 1886.

mid-season form, one's peak form. In *The Indiscretions of Archie* (1921).

mulligatawny, 'in the mulligatawny' is used for 'in the soup', ie 'in trouble'.

niff, to give a disagreeable smell. First recorded in 1927; used by Wodehouse in 1934.

niffiness, recorded only in Wodehouse (1946).

nifty, a joke, witty remark, or story. Apparently coined by Wodehouse in *Carry On, Jeeves!* (1925).

oil off, to go away.

oil out, to back out, withdraw, 'chicken out'.

ooze off, to leave.

pimple, a derogatory term for a person.

pip-pip, goodbye.

pip-squeak, an insignificant person. Recorded before Wodehouse.

pipterino, something good. Possibly unique in Wodehouse.

prune, another derogatory term for a person.

purler, a cropper (as in 'come a cropper').

rannygazoo, horseplay, a trick, caper. The origin is unknown. Variant forms are recorded from at least the turn of the century.

cut up rough, to be angry.

smackers, pounds or dollars.

snifter, a drink; known from the first half of the nineteenth century.

snort, a drink; known at the end of the nineteenth century.

sozzled, squiffy, stewed, drunk.

ten-minute (or twenty-minute egg), a hard-boiled person.
tick, a derogatory term for a person.
tissue-restorer, a drink.
toddle or tool, to go.
old top, used to address a person.
tut-tut, used as a verb.
wart, used of a person.
what-ho, used as a verb.

Wodehouse used words in new senses, changed their parts of speech, formed new compounds, added new affixes, invented circumlocutions, but seldom deviated from known English.

Some of the most interesting and entertaining words are those which are invented or to which no specific meaning can be attached. Foremost among the *creators* of words in English is, of course, the Reverend Charles Lutwidge Dodgson, 'Lewis Carroll'. Many of his most famous verbal creations appear in the poem 'Jabberwocky', in Chapter 1 of *Through the Looking Glass*, and again in *The Hunting of the Snark*. 'Jabberwock' itself is the name of the fabulous monster in the poem, and it clearly is formed on the verb 'to jabber' – to speak volubly and with little sense. Carroll's version of the word early became used to refer to any incoherent or non-sensical expression, so that by 1902 the novelist John Buchan was writing, 'It was the strangest jumble of vowels and conso-nants I had ever met . . . it was some maniac talking jabber-wock to himself.' 'Jabberwocky', too, is widely used for any invented or meaningless language, and even for stupid be-haviour, and both 'jabberwock' and 'jabberwocky' have been used as verbs.

If you want to see how ingenious a genius can be when it comes to originating words, take a really close look at 'Jabberwocky':

> 'Twas brillig, and the slithy toves
> Did gyre and gimble in the wabe:
> All mimsy were the borogoves,
> And the mome raths outgrabe.

What's it all about? Well, nothing and everything, of course. If you'll forgive me for sounding like an earnest American academic – and in this rather special context I do hope you will – let's take a look at the poem, almost word by word:

brillig. In Chapter 6 of *Through the Looking Glass* Humpty Dumpty takes it upon himself to explain the meaning of *Jabberwocky* to Alice. He says, '*Brillig* means four o'clock in the afternoon – the time when you begin *broiling* things for dinner,' and this is much the same as the explanation given by Carroll in an earlier draft of the first stanza: '*Bryllyg* (derived from the verb to *bryl* or *broil*), "the time of broiling dinner, ie the close of the afternoon".'

slithy. This is a classic example of the 'portmanteau word' with two meanings packed into one. Humpty Dumpty says that '*slithy* means "lithe and slimy"' and explains that '"lithe" is the same as "active"'. This is identical to Carroll's earlier explanation: '*Slithy* compounded of *slimy* and *lithe*). "Smooth and active".' In the preface to *The Hunting of the Snark*, Carroll tells us that 'the "i" in "slithy" is long, as in "writhe".' The *Oxford English Dictionary* does record one use of a word *slithy* in 1622, which it suggests may be a variant of 'sleathy', another rare word meaning 'slovenly' or 'careless', but there is no reason to believe that Carroll knew of its existence or that he made up *slithy* in any other way than that stated.

toves. Toves, according to Humpty Dumpty, 'are something like badgers – they're something like lizards – and they're something like corkscrews', and he volunteers the further information: 'also they make their nests under sundials – also they live on cheese'. This is similar in outline to, though different in detail from, Carroll's earlier description: 'a species of Badger. They had smooth white hair, long hind legs, and short horns like a stag; lived chiefly on cheese'. The inspiration for the word is unknown, though we do know that it should be pronounced to rhyme with 'groves' because we are told so in the preface to *The Hunting of the Snark*.

gyre. Humpty Dumpty tells Alice that 'To *gyre* is to go round and round like a gyroscope'. This is the normal meaning of the verb, which is recorded by the *Oxford English Dictionary* from 1420, though Carroll's original explanation of the word was completely different: '*Gyre*, verb (derived from *gyaour* or *giaour*, 'a dog'). "To scratch like a dog".'

gimble. 'To *gimble* is to make holes like a gimlet', according to Humpty Dumpty, and he here agrees with Carroll's first explanation: '*Gymble* (whence *gimblet*). "To screw out holes in anything".' The *OED* records another word *gimble*, a nineteenth-century variant of 'gimbal' (usually 'gimbals', a device for hanging up articles at sea so that they stay in a horizontal position), but there appears to be no connection with the Carroll word. The pronunciation is probably different. Carroll's *gimble*, if derived from 'gimlet', would be pronounced with *g−* as in *go*, whereas the *g* in *gimbal* is pronounced as in *generous*.

wabe. The wabe, as Alice rightly guesses, is the grass plot round a sundial, frequented by toves. Humpty Dumpty reports that 'It's called *wabe* . . . because it goes a long way before it, and a long way behind it – ' and Alice adds 'And a long way beyond it on each side', so that *wabe* is presented as a sort of multiple portmanteau word, from:

$$way + \begin{matrix} be\text{fore} \\ be\text{hind} \\ be\text{yond} \end{matrix}$$

This is a more satisfactory and convincing explanation than that which Carroll originally put forward: '*Wabe* (derived from the verb to *swab* or *soak*). "The side of a hill" (from its being *soaked* by the rain).'

mimsy. This is another portmanteau, says Humpty Dumpty, from 'flimsy and miserable'. Carroll's earlier gloss was 'unhappy'. This may be how mimsy was formed, but there was already an identical dialect word in existence, which Carroll may have known. It meant 'prim' or 'prudish'.

borogoves. 'A *borogove* is a thin shabby-looking bird with its feathers sticking out all round – something like a live mop,' explains Humpty Dumpty. Earlier it had been described as 'An extinct kind of parrot. They had no wings, beaks turned up, and made their nests under sundials; lived on veal.' (In *Through the Looking Glass* it is the toves, of course, who make their nests under sundials.) In the preface to *The Hunting of the Snark*, Carroll tells us that 'the first "o" in *borogoves* is pronounced like the "o" in "borrow". I have heard people try to give it the sound of the "o" in "worry". Such is Human Perversity.'

mome. Humpty Dumpty admits to having trouble with the meaning of mome, but thinks that 'it's short "from home" – meaning that they'd lost their way, you know'. 'Lost' is not what Carroll's earlier version suggested. There he gave the meaning 'grave', and presented it as an earlier stage in the development of the word 'solemn'; '*Mome* (hence *Solemome, solemone,* and *solemn*).' As with the reinterpretation of 'wabe' the general trend of Carroll's thought is towards favouring 'portmanteau' analyses – in the preface to *The Hunting of the Snark* he even says, 'Humpty Dumpty's theory of two meanings packed into one word like a portmanteau, seems to me the right explanation for all [the hard words in *Jabberwocky*].' The *OED* records several different *momes* – one meaning an aunt, another a blockhead, a third a carping critic or a buffoon, and a fourth a variant of a dialect word *malm* meaning 'soft', but nearly all these are obsolete and have no connection with the Carroll *mome*.

rath. 'A *rath*', according to Humpty Dumpty, 'is a sort of green pig,' though Carroll first described it as 'A species of land turtle. Head erect: mouth like a shark: forelegs curved out so that the animal walked on its knees: smooth green body: lived on swallows and oysters'. The *OED* records one word *rath*, Irish by origin, defined as 'an enclosure (usually of a circular form) made by a strong earthen wall, and serving as a fort and place of residence for the chief of a tribe; a hill-fort'.

outgrabe. Humpty Dumpty tells Alice that '*outgribing* is something between bellowing and whistling, with a kind of sneeze in the middle'. Carroll earlier saw it as a different kind of noise: '*Outgrabe*, past tense of the verb to *outgribe*. It is connected with the old verb to *grike*, or *shrike*, from which are derived "shriek" and "creak".' These etymologies are purely fanciful, of course,

    Beware the Jabberwock, my son!
    The jaws that bite, the claws that catch!
    Beware the Jubjub bird, and shun
    The frumious Bandersnatch.

jabberwock. This is formed from the verb 'to jabber' as mentioned earlier. The origin of −*wock* is less clear. In a letter referring to the word Lewis Carroll mentions the Old English word *wocor* meaning 'offspring', but whether he had this in mind when he coined the word is uncertain.

jubjub. The *Supplement to the OED* defines this as 'An imaginary bird of a ferocious, desperate and occasionally charitable nature, noted for its excellence when cooked'. These characteristics are deduced mainly from *The Hunting of the Snark*, in which the Jubjub bird also figures. The most plausible theories about the origin of the word are that it is formed after such representations of bird-cry as *jug-jug* or that it is a portmanteau word from *jabber* and *jujube* (a fruit, or a lozenge flavoured with, or like, the fruit). There may be also some suggestion of *hubbub*.

frumious. Carroll himself gives a full analysis of this word in the preface to *The Hunting of the Snark*. 'Take the two words "fuming" and "furious",' he says. 'Make up your mind that you will say both words, but leave it unsettled which you will say first. Now open your mouth and speak. If your thoughts incline ever so little towards "fuming", you will say "fuming-furious"; if they turn, even by a hair's breadth, towards "furious", you will say "furious-fuming"; but if you have that rarest of gifts, a perfectly balanced mind, you will say *frumious*.'

bandersnatch. Again the definition in the *Supplement to the OED* provides a good summary: 'A fleet, furious, fuming, fabulous creature, of dangerous propensities, immune to bribery and too fast to flee from.' Such is the way the bandersnatch reveals itself in *The Hunting of the Snark*. The word has since been used to suggest any creature with these qualities: for instance, C S Lewis wrote, 'No one ever influenced Tolkien – you might as well try to influence a bandersnatch.' It is presumably a portmanteau word.

vorpal. Carroll appears to have had nothing specific in mind when he coined this word, and once wrote to one of the children with whom he corresponded, 'I am afraid I can't explain *vorpal blade* for you'.

> He took his vorpal sword in hand:
> Long time the manxome foe he sought –
> So rested he by the Tumtum tree,
> And stood awhile in thought.

manxome. The second part of this word is presumably meant to suggest the suffix *−some* found in 'fearsome', 'gruesome', 'loathsome', etc. It is not known if 'Manx', the epithet for the Isle of Man, had any influence in the invention of the word. The *Supplement to the OED* tentatively suggests the general sense 'fearsome'.

tumtum. The *OED* entry for this word says 'An imitation of the sound of a stringed instrument or instruments, esp[ecially] when monotonously played.' There could also be a suggestion of such childish words for 'stomach' as 'tummy' and its variants.

uffish. Carroll himself once wrote that this word implied 'a state of mind when the voice is gruffish, the manner roughish, and the temper huffish'.

> And, as in uffish thought he stood
> The Jabberwock, with eyes of flame,
> Came whiffling through the tulgey wood.
> And burbled as it came.

whiffling. The *OED* records a number of meanings for the intransitive use of this verb: (i) 'To blow in puffs or slight gusts, also used figuratively with the sense "to vacillate, to be variable or evasive".' (ii) 'To move lightly as if blown by a puff of air; to flicker or flutter as if stirred by the wind.' (iii)

'To talk idly, to trifle – a dialectal use.' (iv) 'To make a light whistling sound.'

tulgey. This is another word that Carroll found himself unable to explain.

burble. This is possibly a blend of 'burst' and 'bubble', though Carroll wrote of an alternative suggestion: 'If you take the three verbs "*b*leat", "m*ur*mur", and "war*ble*", and select the bits I have underlined, it certainly makes *burble*; though I am afraid I can't distinctly remember having made it in that way.' *Burble*, an onomatopoeic word meaning to flow in or with bubbles, or to flow with a bubbling sound, etc was used from the beginning of the fourteenth century – in fact earlier than 'bubble' itself – and during the fifteenth and sixteenth centuries. There is also evidence of a Scottish word *burble* meaning to confuse or muddle. The *Supplement to the OED* records late nineteenth- and early twentieth-century examples of *burble* meaning to speak or say something murmurously or in a rambling manner, and it is likely that the word was given a new lease of life by the burbling of the Jabberwock.

snicker-snack. Both *snick* and *snack* appear in the *OED* as verbs meaning to snip or snap.

> One, two! One, two! And through and through
> The vorpal blade went snicker-snack!
> He left it dead, and with its head
> He went galumphing back.

galumph. This is one of the Jabberwocky words which has passed into general currency. The *OED* suggests reminiscence of *gallop* and triumphant, and defines it as 'To march exultingly with irregular bounding movements', while the *Supplement* adds 'Now usu[ally] to gallop heavily; to bound or move clumsily or noisily'.

Heart Attack!

beamish. The *OED* gives the meaning as 'shining brightly' and cites Carroll's use, and one other dated 1530, and describes the word as archaic.

> And hast thou slain the Jabberwock?
> Come to my arms, my beamish boy!
> O frabjous day! Callooh! Callay!
> He chortled in his joy.

frabjous. This adjective is apparently intended to suggest 'fair' and 'joyous'. This also has been taken up by others – including Rudyard Kipling and Dorothy Sayers – and converted to an adverb 'frabjously'.

callooh! callay!. The *OED* mentions *calloo* as the name of an

Arctic duck, presumably so named from its call. There are also suggestions of other interjections such as 'halloo' and 'horray'. However, it has been suggested that *callooh! callay!* represents a phonetic rendering of two forms of a Greek word meaning 'beautiful' or 'good', and this would be appropriate here.

chortle. This word was taken up by others almost immediately. The *OED* records an example from 1876, only four years after the publication of *Through the Looking Glass*. Though intransitive in 'Jabberwocky', it has since also been used as a transitive verb, and converted into a noun. It is aparently a blend of 'chuckle' and 'snort'.

Lewis Carroll loved words and had a lot of fun with them. Even if we lack his genius, we can always attempt to ape his ingenuity. Creating 'portmanteau' words is an entertaining pastime and here are some favourites of mine taken from a book on American slang:

beautility	beauty + utility
censcissors	beauty + scissors
drizzerable	drizzle + miserable
exaccurate	exact + accurate
expectacle	expect + spectacle
extreamline	extreme + streamline
feduppity	fed up + uppity
feebility	feeble + debility
fride	free + ride
gawkward	gawky + awkward
grandy	grand + dandy
guesstimate	guess + estimate
happenident	happen + accident
heartistic	heart + artistic
identicate	identify + indicate
impitate	imp + imitate
jummix	jumble + mix
limpsy	limp + flimsy
numberal	number + numeral
obliviation	oblivion + obliteration

prevusical	preview + musical
promptual	prompt + punctual
prounce	prance + flounce
ritzycratic	ritzy + aristocratic
scrumple(d)	squeeze + crumple(d)
scrush	squash + crush
shamateur	sham + amateur
sizzard	sizzle + blizzard
skreaky	screechy + creaky
slickery	slick + slippery
slich	slice + slash
squnch	squeeze + crunch
strivation	starve-starvation + privation
stuffocation	stuffy + suffocation
superplace	supersede + replace
surfooded	surfeited + food
swelegant	swell + elegant
torrible	terrible + horrible
tumoil	tumult + turmoil
whurtle	whirl + hurtle

Most of these jocular blends would not find their way into standard dictionaries, though the words 'scrumple' and 'swelegant' may have passed your lips and 'guesstimate' has gained a very wide currency.

Other portmanteau favourites of mine that have found their way into the *OED* and its Supplements include:

anecdotard, from anecdote + dotard, a dotard given to telling anecdotes, first found in 1894 and used by Rudyard Kipling in 1937.

bingle, from bob + shingle, a short hairstyle for women, first recorded in 1925. It also occurs as a verb.

botel, from boat + hotel, a hotel catering for boat owners (1956) or a ship with hotel facilities (1959).

brunch, from breakfast + lunch, a meal taken late in the morning. The first recorded example is from 1896.

cheeseburger, from cheese + hamburger, recorded from 1938.

Chunnel, a projected tunnel under the English Channel, first found in 1928 and soon to be a reality.

citrange, from citrus + orange, a hybrid fruit (1904).

liger, from lion + tiger, the offspring of a lion and a tigress. The first written record is in 1938.

macon, from mutton + bacon. This was mutton salted and smoked like bacon, eaten during World War II. The first recorded example is November 1939.

mocamp, from motor + camp. An area providing parking and camping facilities. The first example is from 1967.

moondoggle, a slang blend of moon and boondoggle (a trivial undertaking, wasteful expenditure), found from 1962.

motel, one of the best known of recent blends, from motor + hotel. It is first recorded in 1925.

Naussie, from new + Aussie (Australian), a recent immigrant to Australia, usually from Europe, first found in 1959.

Nobodaddy, a blend of nobody and daddy, used by the poet William Blake (*c* 1793) and others after him as a disrespectful name for God.

If you've got nothing much to do between now and midnight, why not follow in the footsteps of William Blake – or Lewis Carroll or P G Wodehouse – and invent a word? Gluck!

Old World, New Words

On the next few pages you'll find long lists of words, some old, some new, all of them, I trust, intriguing. From the lists of old words you'll discover how ancient much of your everyday vocabulary is and you may even be tempted to enrich it by adopting some of the splendid-sounding old words that have become obsolete. And from the lists of new words you'll discover how many of our modern terms and expressions have been created and may even be inspired to start coining an original vocabulary of your own.

Old Words

As a rule words have life spans much greater than those of people. A youngster today may regard a word adopted in the nineteenth century – or the last decade's slang – as old, but in terms of linguistic history the words are youngsters themselves. I class as really 'old' any words which are recorded in the language before 1500, that is to say words found in Old and Middle English. These include some of our most familiar words, and some that are completely unknown.

Words recorded in Old-English texts have met a variety of fates. Many have survived with sense virtually unchanged into the twentieth century; others have lived on, but with modified meaning. Some failed to outlive even the Old English period; others became obsolete in Middle English or shortly afterwards; many others, though obsolete in standard English, live on in dialectal use. To give you an idea of the extent and nature of these classes I'll run through the alphabet giving a few examples of each.

Old-English Words

A

We still have, for example: acre, after, all, altar, answer, apple, arm and ask. Long obsolete are:

adle, sickness, disease
adle, to be diseased
ae, a river
ae, law
are, honour, clemency
are, to show grace, clemency, respect
arm, poor, needy
athel, noble
atheling, a noble person (though this word is still found in histories of the Old-English period)
atol, dire, terrible
attor, poison

B

Still very much with us are, for instance: back, bath, be, bear, beat, bed, bench, bind, bishop, bite, bitter, black, blind, bliss, blithe, blood, break, breast, bridge, broad, brother, butter, and busy. Obsolete words include:

beadu, battle
beot, a vow, boast
bigspell, a parable
bismer, insult, disgrace
bode, messenger (obsolete from the twelfth century, but affected by some nineteenth-century writers on Old English history)

C

Survivors include calf, candle, cheese, child, church, cloth, cold, come, and cup. Completely obsolete words include:

chaste, to correct by discipline, rebuke, restraint, etc
chithe, a sprout, a shoot
churl, to take a husband
cof, quick, nimble, eager

Words spelled with a *c* in Old English would now often be spelled with *k* and more words are to be found under that letter; Old English words beginning with *cw−* are now spelled *qu−*.

D

We still have such words as dare, dark, daughter, day, dead, death, deep, devil, dish, do, dog, door, drink and drive. Completely obsolete are, for example:

dighel, secret, obscure
dolg, a wound
douth, virtue, nobility
drast, *drest*, dregs, lees
dright, a host, an army
drightin, *−ten*, a lord, ruler

E

Some words still in use are ear, earnest, earth, east, edge, end, evening and evil. Some obsolete words are:

eche, everlasting, eternal
eche, to enlarge, increase
echelich, eternal
eddre, a blood vessel, vein
eftersoons, again, soon

ellen, courage, zeal
erd, native land
erde, to dwell, live
erding, abode, dwelling
este, favour, grace, pleasure
ethem, vapour, breath

F

Hardy survivors include fair, fall, fat, father, feather, feed, fetter, fight, filth, finger, fire, fish, floor, flow, foe, folk and friend. Victims of time include:

facenfull, treacherous
fasten, fortress
fastrede, firm in purpose, inflexible
fax, the hair of the head
faxed, hairy, having hair
felefold, many times over, by a great deal
ferd, an army, host
ferding, military expedition
firen, flaming with fire
fordilghe, to exterminate, destroy
fordit, to shut or stop up
fracod, wicked
frede, to feel, perceive
freke, a warrior, champion, man
frith, peace (though this word occurs in some histories
    of the period)
frover, comfort
frume, beginning
fullought, baptism

G

Still with us are such words as give, glide, glove, go, God, gold, good, greedy and green. We have, however, lost such words as:

knuckle-duster...

gavel, payment, tribute (though this occurs in some
history books)

gome, a man

gong, a privy

greme, to anger, vex

grith, protection, security (another word sometimes
taken up by history writers)

gristbiting, gnashing of teeth

H

Still everyday words are, for instance: hand, have, heat, heath, heathen, heaven, hell, help, hew, high, hoard, hold, home, horse, hound, house and hunger. Long obsolete vocabulary includes:

here, a host, multitude
hetol, hostile
heven, to raise, lift
hightly, joyous, hopeful
hild, war
hux, scorn, derision

I

Familiar today are idle, inn, iron, etc. Unfamiliar to most, as now obsolete, are, for example:

inbring, to bring in
inc, you two, both of you
inker (genitive dual) of you two, of both of you
iwene, to expect, hope
iwill, will, wish, pleasure
iwin, labour, toil, battle
iwit, knowledge, wits

J

This was not an independent letter in Old and Middle English but was used as a variant of *i*.

K

This was a rare letter in Old English, *c* being used in words which we now spell with *k*. Under this letter in the *OED* can be found everyday words such as king, kiss, and know. Obsolete words include:

> *kechel*, a little cake
> *ken*, to generate, give birth to
> *kindom*, kingdom

Survivors of limited currency are, for example:

> *keel*, to cool (still used in some dialects)
> *kemb*, to disentangle and smooth (hair) (also still used in some dialects)
> *kemp*, warrior, champion (in dialectal use)
> *knape*, obsolete in the OE sense 'a male child', but still used as a term of contempt in some dialects.

L

In constant use are still, for example, lamb, land, law, lead, learning, leave, life, light, little, liver, long, love and lust. No longer used are such words as:

> *larew*, a teacher
> *latemost*, last
> *lease*, untrue, false; also, an untruth, lying
> *leech-finger*, a finger next to the little finger
> *leoth*, a song
> *licham*, the body

limp, to befall, happen
limphalt, lame, limping
lodeman, a leader, guide, pilot
lof, praise
love, to praise, extol
lovely, lovingly, affectionately
lovewende, beloved, loving
lout, to lurk, sneak

M

Still with us are, for example, maiden, man, many, martyr, mass, mead, meat, middle, might, mild, misdeed, mist, month, moor, moth and mother. Obsolete are such words as:

mathele, to speak, talk, prate
mere, renowned, illustrious, beautiful
mette, a companion at meat
mid, with
mithe, to conceal, dissemble (feelings, etc)
mone, companionship

N

Words still current in standard English include nail, name, need, never, new, night, noon, north, and now. Among obsolete words we find, for example:

nithe, envy, malice, hatred
nitheful, envious, malicious
norther, further north, more northerly
nutte, to use, make use of

Now only in specialized uses are, for instance:

nesh, to become soft, to make soft (obsolete except in
  a dialectal expression 'to nesh it', meaning to 'turn
  faint-hearted')
nicker, a water-demon (still sometimes used as a
  conscious archaism)
nim, to take (also occasionally found as an archaism)

O

Survivors from Old English now spelled with *o*– are such words as oar, oath, old, open, other, oven, over, and ox. Among the numerous obsolete terms are:

ofdrede, to terrify, frighten
ord, a point, spear
ovemest, highest, topmost

P

Still in use are, for example, penny, play, pope, post, pound and priest. Obsolete terms include:

pell, a skin, hide; a skin or roll of parchment (still, however, found in some historical writing)
portic, a porch, portico
prass, proud array, pomp

Q

Old English used *cw*– where we now use *qu*–, but under this letter in the *OED* are found such words as queen. Among those which have fallen into disuse are:

quale, death, destruction, mortality
quethe, to speak, declare
quide, a saying, speech; a legacy, bequest

R

Old English *r*– words still in use include ram, reach, reading, reek, rest, ride, right and rope. No longer current are such words as:

rathely, quickly
rec(c)he, to tell, narrate, say
rechelest, rechelust, carelessness, negligence
riche, rike, kingdom, royal power
rine, to rain, to fall like rain
rouner, a whisperer, tale-bearer
rune, course, onward movement
ryen, made from rye

S

We still use such words as salt, sea, seed, sell, send, sight, silver, sing, sit, shaft, shame, sharp, shave, sheep, shilling, shine, ship, short, shower, sleep, snow, son, song, sorrow, sorry, soul, south, spark, spear, spring, stake, stand, steep, stench, stillness, storm, stream, street, strong, summer, sun, swear, sweet and swift. We have lost, for example:

sale, a hall, a spacious chamber
samed, together
samening, a gathering, assembly
segge, a man
shaft, creation; a creature
shipe, wages, reward
shond, shame, scandal
sithe, a going, journey, path
sithen, after, seeing that
smicker, beautiful, elegant
smolt, lard, fat
snoter, wise, learned, skilful
soot, sweet
souther, more southerly; situated to the south
stathel, to place on a foundation; to establish
stathelfast, firm, steadfast
steven, time, turn, vicissitude, occasion
such, as if
swench, affliction, trial, labour, toil

swenche, to trouble, harass
sweng, a stroke, a blow
swepe, to scourge, whip
swerk, to become dark; to become gloomy or sad
sweve, to sleep
sweven, to dream
swikedom, deceit, fraud, treachery
swime, dizziness, a swoon
swind, to waste away, languish

T

Vigorous as ever are, for example, teach, tear, time, tongue, tool, tooth, tread, tree and turf. No longer used are such words as:

tealt, unsteady, insecure, shaky
tee, to accuse
teen, to vex, enrage
teld, a tent, pavilion
teld, to spread, set up
tele, evil speaking, calumny
tharf, need, necessity
thede, a people, race, nation
thee, to grow, thrive, prosper
thrinness, threefold condition; the Trinity
throw, to suffer, bear, endure
thrum, a company, band, troop
tidder, to be productive or prolific
tintregh, torment, torture
trume, a body of persons, especially of troops
twie, twice
twilly, twilled
twirede, of two minds, undecided

U

Among the many Old English words still in use are uncouth, under, up, and many other words beginning in *un−*. Obsolete terms include:

underfo, to receive, to undertake
unfere, infirm, weak
unmight, weakness, feebleness
unmild, harsh, rough, unkind
unsoft, severely
untime, an unsuitable time
untrum, weak, ailing
unweather, bad, rough, or stormy weather
unworth, unworthy
uvemest, uppermost, highest
unveward, upper, higher

V

Neither the letter *v* nor the sound represented by it is found at the beginning of a word in Old English.

W

Among the many words still in use are wall, warp, watch, water, wax, way, weapon, weary, west, wide, wife, will, wind, windy, wine, winter, wisdom, wise, wolf, wonder, word, world and wound. Among obsolete words are:

waldend, a ruler, governor
werde, to harm, injure
were, a male person, a man
wered, a troop, band, host
winly, pleasant, agreeable
wissing, guidance, direction, instruction
witherward, hostile, inimical
withgo, to go against, oppose
witword, testament
wlating, loathing, abhorrence
wlite, beauty, splendour
wlonk, proud, haughty
wurp, a (stone's) throw
wye, a fighting man, a warrior or soldier

X

Words having initial *x*– in English are nearly all of Greek origin.

Y

This letter has a complex history which I can't go into here but you can read 10,000 fascinating words on the subject in vol. 12 of the *Oxford English Dictionary*. Old English words now written with *y*– include yard, yawn, yea, year, yearn, yellow, yelp, yes, yesterday, you and young. Osbolete Old English words found under *y* in the *Oxford English Dictionary* include:

yain, to meet, encounter
yark, to make ready, prepare, oppose
yclepe, to call by name
yepe, cunning, sly
yern, to run
yerne, eagerly, diligently
yfere, a companion, associate
yisse, to covet
yoklet, a small manor
yong, to go
ythe, a wave of the sea
ywhere, everywhere

Z

This letter was used in Old English only in the spelling of alien words and in certain loan words. It derives its form through the medium of the Latin and Greek alphabets, from the Phoenician and Ancient Hebrew IIZ. A survival is *zephyr*: *OE* 'the god of the westwind'.

Middle-English Words

The Middle-English period saw a great influx of words into English, mainly from French, and also the formation of many new words from native resources. However, great numbers of these failed to outlive the Middle-English period. Here are some of the words recorded in the *Oxford English Dictionary* only at some point between 1000 and 1500:

A

abound, overflowing, plentiful
acast, to cast down, to cast off
affect, disposed, inclined
alangeness, tediousness, weariness, loneliness
anburst, to burst out
apparissaunt, apparent, evident
arund, to rail at, revile, scold
attribue, to attribute
awem, to corrupt, dishonour
avent, to air, refresh with cold air

B

baisier, a kiss, kissing
barrenty, barrenness
bedoubt, to dread
berling, a little bear, bear's cub
bimong, among
blethely, graciously, blithely
bleyke, pale; to become pale
bourd, to joust, tilt
bremely, fierce, furious
brust, bristled, bristling

C

caterve, a band, company
chancely, by chance

chapitle, chapter
chaple, a fierce combat or encounter
chargeant, burdensome, onerous
charitous, charitable
charnel, carnal
chartre, a prison
chasty, to correct, chasten
chel, throat
chenaille, canaille, rabble
chooseling, a chosen one

D

darkhede, darkness
derf, trouble, tribulation
dold, stupid, inert
dought, doughty, valiant
drunk, to drench, make drunken
dryhede, dryness, drought

E

erite, a heretic

F

faciale, a face-cloth for a corpse
facrere, the art of make-believe, deception
fade, strong, brave, large
fastship, parsimony
ferd, fear, terror
ferdlac, state of fear, terror
forfret, to devour, gnaw
forgettingness, forgetfulness

G

gain, advantage, remedy, help
gitterner, a player on the gittern
graith, prepared, ready
graithful, prompt, speedy
grame, to displease
grindel, fierce, angry
gristbite, gnashing of teeth

H

hethely, scornfully
het(t)erly, roughly, violently, keenly
heven, to take vengeance
hightle, to adorn, ornament
hofles, immoderate, intemperate
hute, outcry

I

iwhiles, in the meantime
iwil, pleasant, agreeable
iwon, iwan, hope, expectation
iworded, talkative

J

jamby, strong in the legs
jealouste, jealousy, zeal
jobard, a stupid fellow, a fool
jovencel, a young man, a youth
joyingly, joyfully

K

keb, to boast, brag
keenship, boldness, keenness
kench, to laugh loudly
kip, to take hold of, seize, snatch
knurned, knotted, rugged, gnarled

L

lateful, late in season
lateship, slowness, sluggishness
lech, a look, glance
lettrure, written book, story, learning
liche, form, figure, guise
lichy, like
lodder, wretched
lote, to forsake, fail
lothen, shaggy
love-worth, loveworthy

M

madship, madness
mainful, powerful, mighty
medlure, mixing, mixture
mere, a mother
mire, an ant
mone, to remember, bear in mind

N

nesebek, a dish in medieval cookery
nice, a foolish or simple person
nithe, to (feel) envy
nutrix, nurse, rearer

O

ofdrunken, to drown, swallow up in water
onelihede, solitude; unity
onfast, near, fast by
oning, an only one, darling
orcost, penury, want of means

P

paliure, a thorny shrub
pelleter, wild or garden thyme
perer, a pear-tree
poperiche, popedom
porture, bearing, behaviour
prank, a pleat, fold
punct, to appoint
putrede, rotting, putridity

Q

quain, to lament, bewail
quaintise, wisdom, cleverness
quatreme, a duty or tax of the fourth part
quarer, quarry
quest, a bequest
quinible, fivefold, quintuple

R

rechase, to recheat
recheles-ship, recklessness
rich, to tug, pull

rodewort, the marigold
roll, to polish, burnish
rudesse, rudeness
ruel-bone, ivory
runge, to rise up
runish, fierce, violent
rynmart, an ox or cow paid as part of a rent in kind (a
    Scottish word)

S

saler, a salt cellar
samentale, concord, agreement
samly, agreeingly
scogh, a wood
seele, a canopy
seem, seemly, proper, fitting
seynt, a girdle
skleir, a veil
slipe, to make smooth, polish
snode, a morsel
socie, to associate, ally, join
sol, soiled, dirty
some, united, reconciled
South-end, the South of England
spender, a steward
spreth, frail, liable to sin
strathely, steadfast, firm
stew, to check, restrain
stith, to set firmly
sturb, to trouble, upset
suchkin, of such a kind
swelm, the heat of anger or the like

T

tharn, to be without, lack, need
thethen, from that place, thence

thewful, good, virtuous, moral
thrimness, the Trinity
thring, a crowd, throng of people
tine, a vessel for brewing, a tub, vat
tutel, to whisper
twilighting, twilight

U

uncunning, ignorance
underbring, to bring into subjection
unhend, discourteous, impolite
unnait, useless, unprofitable
unsoft, hard, severe
unworship, to deprive of honour or dignity
unsant, accustomed (to do something)

V

vallente, power, might
ventose, to bleed (a patient) by means of a cupping glass
verrer, a glazier
vesteye, to inspect, examine
voutry, adultery

W

wawy, full of waves, billowy
waynpain, a sort of gauntlet
ween, beautiful
wisehede, wisdom

wisser, a leader, guide
withsaw, withsaying
wlaffe, to stammer, speak indistinctly
wlat, loathsome, detestable
wlatsome, loathsome, detestable
wumme, woe is me!
wunsele, a dwelling place
wyring, a small strong rope for tying a sail

Y

yeder, quick, frequent
yei, a wail, cry
yemelich, full of care, anxious
yemsel, keeping care, custody, charge
yeting, casting of metal or a metal object
yhere, obedient
younghede, youth
ysee, to behold

Z

Most words with *z*– date from after the Middle-English period.

I can only touch the surface of Old- and Middle-English vocabulary here, so you may be interested to know where you can pursue the subject further. The standard Old-English Dictionary used by specialists is: *An Anglo-Saxon dictionary based on the manuscript collections of the late Joseph Bosworth . . . edited and enlarged by T Northcote Toller* (popularly known as 'Bosworth and Toller') which appeared between 1882 and 1892. Toller produced a *Supplement* to this

Background...

work in 1921, and more recently (1972), *Enlarged Addenda and Corrigenda to the Supplement by T Northcote Toller* was published by the late Professor Alistair Campbell. Shorter works more within the range (and pocket) of the beginner include *A Concise Anglo-Saxon Dictionary* by John R Clark Hall, now in its fourth edition, with a *Supplement*, by Herbert D Meritt (1960), and *The Student's Dictionary of Anglo-Saxon* by Henry Sweet, first published in 1896 and reprinted many times since. There are also glossaries at the back of such standard works as *Sweet's Anglo-Saxon Reader* and in editions of individual Old English poems, etc.

Middle English is much more heterogeneous than Old English. Spelling varies greatly from manuscript to manuscript according to period, dialect, training (or whim) of the scribe, and this makes the preparation of a Middle-English dictionary a formidable task. The huge Middle-English dictionary in progress at the University of Michigan is only into

the letter M at the time of writing, and it is much too complicated for the non-specialist to use. One of the few available
completed Middle-English dictionaries is *A Middle-English
Dictionary* by Francis Henry Stratmann, rearranged, revised
and enlarged by Henry Bradley. The glossaries of such standard student readers as *Early Middle-English Verse and Prose*
by J A W Bennett and G V Smithers and *Fourteenth-Century
Verse and Prose* by Kenneth Sisam are probably therefore the
most accessible lists of Middle-English vocabulary. For the
fourteenth century you can also look at James Orchard Halli-
well's *A Dictionary of Archaic and Provincial Words* a nineteenth-century work which has gone through a number of
editions.

New Words

The twentieth century has seen the addition of enormous
numbers of words to the English language, probably more
than in any previous century. Science and technology account
largely, but by no means wholly, for this expansion – a glance
through the *Supplement to the Oxford English Dictionary* will
reveal the proliferation of slang and other specialized uses of
language. The twentieth century is also marked by disturb-
ances in the traditional methods of word formation, disturb-
ances which are frequently unwelcome to philologists.

In previous centuries the main sources of new vocabulary
have been the adoption of foreign loan words and the joining
together of existing English elements, adding a prefix (*a*–,
de–, *mis*–, *pre*–, *re*–, *un*–, etc) at the beginning of a
word, a suffix (*–al*, *–ize*, *–y*, etc) at the ending of a word, or
putting two words together. These are still the most common
methods of forming new words, but to them have been added
methods which defeat the application of traditional etymological principles in discovering word origins – acronyms and
initialisms, the arbitrary combination of syllables from different words, even anagrams. Science and technology are the
chief offenders here.

For the sake of simplicity I am defining a 'new word' as one which is first recorded in the *Supplement to the OED* in written use in or after 1914. All such cut-off points are to a certain extent arbitrary, but the date 1914 makes it likely that the new words recorded genuinely belong to the twentieth century, since words are frequently current in spoken language for a few years before they are written down, while it doesn't exclude the creative slang of World War I. Each word will be followed by the date of the first example in the *Supplement to the OED*, and some by an explanation of meaning, though I have made no attempt to define many scientific words, this often being impossible without recourse to even more abstruse vocabulary.

First, suffixes – elements appended to words, usually to change the part of speech, make a noun into a verb, an adjective into an adverb, etc. The following alphabetical list does not include *all* productive English suffixes, but many of the common suffixes are illustrated, and I think they will give you an idea of how this method of word formation works.

−able. This is freely added to words, with a passive sense; 'that can, may, must be −d', 'that can be made the subject of', or 'that is relevant to or in accordance with':

    afforestable 1928
    bombable 1930
    filmable 1920
    hummable 1941
    hydratable 1953
    immortable (having the capacity to live after death) 1922
    jeepable (negotiable by jeep) 1944
    leapable 1925

−acy. Forming nouns of state or quality:

    articulacy 1934

−*age*. Forming nouns with various senses, including 'product of an action', 'function or condition', and 'aggregate or number of':

frettage (damage suffered by two metal surfaces when
    clamped or otherwise held together, owing to
    slight relative motion to and fro) 1938
headage (the number of animals) 1957
hourage 1924

−*al*. Forming adjectives, usually from nouns:

behavioural *c* 1927
genocidal 1948
improvisational 1923
libidinal 1922
neocolonial 1961

−*an*. Forming adjectives and nouns, especially from names of places, people, and systems:

Gerzean (from El Gerzeh, a district in Egypt; used as
    the adjective of pre-Dynastic Egyptian culture)
    1925
Hemingwayan (from the name of the American
    novelist Ernest Hemingway) 1957

−*ant*. Forming nouns, and occasionally adjectives, usually implying an action − used for doing or causing something:

attractant 1926
dispersant 1944
euphoriant 1947
incapacitant 1961

−*ary*. Forming adjectives, meaning 'connected with, pertaining to':

illocutionary
locutionary
perlocutionary

terms used by the philosopher
J L Austin in 1955

−*ate*. There are several suffixes with this form:

1　Forming nouns:
avunculate (in anthropology, the name for a special
　　relationship existing in some societies between a
　　maternal uncle and his sister's son) 1920
barbiturate 1928

2　Forming adjectives:
axiate (from axis) 1926
illatinate (having no knowledge of Latin; modelled
　　after illiterate) 1922
linguate (tongue-shaped) 1940

3　Forming verbs:
desalinate 1949
fluorinate 1931
hydroxylate 1951

−*ation*. Forming nouns where there is no corresponding
verb in −*ate* at the time of coining; denoting a verbal action
or an instance of this, or the state or thing resulting from an
action:

automatization 1924
devaluation 1914

implementation 1926
metrication (suggested by E McIntosh of the Oxford
    dictionaries) 1965

−*centric*. Forming adjectives, meaning 'having (such) a centre' or 'having a specified centre' or, in biology, 'having the centromere attached at a specified point'.

accentric 1937
acrocentric (of a chromosome) 1945
logocentric (centred on reason) 1939

−*cide*. Forming nouns meaning 'person or substance that kills' or 'killing of':

biocide (destruction of body tissue; also, a pesticide)
    1947
genocide 1944
menticide (coined by J A M Meerloo for a type of
    brain-washing) 1951
miticide (for killing mites) 1946

−*cy*. Forming abstract nouns:

inarticulacy 1921

−*cyte*. Forming nouns with the meaning 'cell':

athrocyte (a cell having the property of absorbing and
    retaining solid particles) 1938

knee
cap.

−don. Forming nouns with the meaning 'condition, state, dignity', 'domain, realm', or with the meaning of a collective plural or 'the ways of (a specified group)':

Arabdom 1949
gangdom 1926
gangsterdom 1923
middle-classdom 1939
Nazidom 1933

−*dyne*. Used in the formation of scientific, especially electrical, terms and meaning 'power':

    autodyne 1918
    neutrodyne 1923

−*ectomy*. Used to form words denoting a surgical operation for the removal of a part:

    ganglionectomy 1925
    hymenectomy 1931
    mastectomy (a breast) 1923

−*ed*. There are two suffixes with this form:

    1 Forming participial adjectives from verbs:
    atmosphered 1920
    jazzed (−up) 1919
    landscaped 1927
    Nazified 1934

    2 Forming adjectives from nouns:
    beavered (bearded) 1928
    binoculared 1959
    blazered 1931
    bobbled (ornamented with bobbles) 1955
    bunned (with hair in a bun) 1944

−*ee*. Forming words denoting a party involving in something (frequently a passive party) or a person concerned with or described as:

billet(t)ee 1939
exploitee 1941
mergee 1964
missionee 1951

−*eer*. Forming nouns with the meaning 'one is concerned with' or 'one who deals in', and frequently with derogatory connotations:

allotmenteer (one who holds or rents an allotment of
    land) 1923
fictioneer 1923
junketeer 1939

−*er*. There are a number of suffixes with this form.

1 The principal type forms mainly occupational or
    agent nouns:
beeper 1946
ghoster 1956
go-getter 1921
goose-stepper 1923
grasser (slang for a police informer) 1950
juicer (slang for an electrician) 1928
loner 1947

2 Used to make jocular formations on nouns by
    clipping or curtaining them and adding −*er* to the
    remaining part. It is originally and still chiefly
    school and university slang.
lumpers (a lump sum paid as compensation for loss of
    employment) 1969

−*eroo*. A factitious slang suffix:

boozeroo (New Zealand slang for a drinking spree)
    1943
brusheroo (a brush-off) 1941

−*ery*. (frequently contracted to −*ry*). Forming nouns, usually with the force 'that which is characteristic of, all that is connected with', and also sometimes denoting a place where an employment etc is carried on:

> banditry (the practices of bandits) 1922
> gimmick(e)ry 1952
> Godwottery (an affected or over-elaborate style of
>   gardening, or attitude towards gardens – taken
>   from the line 'A garden is a lovesome thing, God
>   wot!' in T E Browne's poem 'My Garden' 1876)
>   1939
> nitery (American slang for a night club) 1934
> noshery (a restaurant or snack bar) 1963

−*ese*. Forming adjectives and nouns from the names of foreign countries or towns, meaning 'inhabitant or language of' or forming nouns from names of writers denoting 'style of writing':

> Guyanese 1965
> Harlemese 1928
> headlinese 1927
> legalese 1914

−*esque*. Forming adjectives, with the meaning 'resembling the style, partaking of the characteristics of':

> Audenesque (the poet W H Auden) 1940
> Gandhi-esque (the Indian political leader and social
>   reformer M K Gandhi) 1954
> Goyaesque (the Spanish artist Goya) 1934
> Hitleresque 1944

−*ette*. Chiefly forming diminutive nouns, nouns meaning an imitation or substitute, or denoting a female:

beaverette (an imitation beaver fur) 1922
farmerette (a farmeress) 1918
featurette (a short feature film) 1942
luncheonette 1924

−*fication*. Forming nouns of action corresponding to verbs in −*fy*:

Nazification 1933

−*ful*. Forming (1) adjectives meaning 'full of' or, more usually, in the weakened sense, 'having, characterized by'; (2) nouns denoting a receptacle full of something, or the quantity that fills or would fill (a receptacle):

beltful 1916
flavourful (adj) 1927
neckful 1920
nibful 1930

−*genesis*. Used in various quasi-Greek compounds in science, denoting modes of generation:

gynogenesis 1925

−*genic*. Forming adjectives with the meaning 'of pertaining to, or relating to generation or production':

carcinogenic (cancer-producing) 1926
goitrogenic (causing goitre) 1929
iatrogenic (induced unintentionally by a physician) 1924
microgenic (of a voice: well suited to broadcasting) 1931

−gram. Forming nouns denoting something written, etc:

> fathogram (a tracing made by an echo-sounder) 1950
> hologram (a pattern produced by light) 1949
> latrinogram (Services' slang for a baseless rumour
> believed to originate in the latrines) 1944

−graph. Forming nouns, chiefly with the sense 'that which writes, portrays, or records':

> climograph (a graphical representation of the
> differences between different types of climate)
> 1916
> hypsograph (a curve showing the area or proportion of
> the earth's surface above any given elevation or
> depth) 1937

−graphy. Forming nouns denoting processes or style of writing, drawing, or graphic representation:

> flexography (a rotary letterpress technique) 1952
> ionography (in chemistry, the same as
> electrochromatography) 1950

−ia. There are two suffixes with this form used in English:

> 1 Forming abstract nouns, frequently in modern Latin
> terms in pathology:

> achalasia (failure of a muscle to relax) 1914
> anoxia (deficiency of oxygen in the tissues) 1931

> 2 Forming pseudo-Latin plurals:

> militaria (military articles of historical interest) 1964

−ian. Forming adjectives (often used as nouns) with the force 'of or belonging to', particularly in formations from names of persons or places. It is also used to form adjectives in mineralogy:

> Adlerian (the psychologist Alfred Adler) 1933
> Brechtian (the German playwright and poet Bertold
>   Brecht) 1935
> Holmesian (the fictional detective Sherlock Holmes)
>   1929
> Nabokovian (the writer Vladimir Nabokov) 1959

−iana. Forming plural nouns denoting minor works, articles associated with (a specified person), etc:

> Lincolniana (Abraham Lincoln) 1921
> Hitleriana 1966

−ic. One of the most common suffixes forming adjectives (many of which can be used as nouns):

> aleatoric (done at random) 1961
> fascistic 1928
> genic (of genes) 1922

−ician. Denoting a person skilled in an art or science:

> beautician 1924

−icity. Forming abstract nouns from adjectives (usually in *−ic*):

> facticity (factualness) 1945
> monosyllabicity 1951

−*ie*. (see under −*y*)

−*ify*. Used to form verbs:

> aridify 1920
> jazzify 1922
> massify 1954

−*in*. 1 A chemical suffix:

> actinomycin 1940
> ferredoxin 1962

2 The adverb −*in* used as a suffix on the model of 'sit-in' designating a communal act of protest or a large gathering for some common purpose. This is one of the newest suffixes, not yet having been in use for twenty years, and currently very productive:

be-in 1967	read-in 1961
bury-in 1961	shop-in 1965
chain-in 1967	shout-in 1969
cook-in 1961	sing-in 1965
eat-in 1965	sit-in 1960
fish-in 1964	sleep-in 1965
hate-in 1967	stall-in 1963
kiss-in 1968	stand-in 1961
kneel-in 1960	study-in 1961
laugh-in 1968	swim-in 1961
love-in 1967	teach-in 1965
mill-in 1967	wade-in 1960
play-in 1965	walk-in 1970
pray-in 1967	work-in 1970

−ine. A chemical suffix:

> alabamine 1932
> astatine 1947
> glassine 1916
> methionine 1928

−ing. 1 Used to form verbal nouns:

> armouring 1924
> broadcasting 1922
> longshoring 1926
> merchanting 1930

2 Forming participial adjectives:

> arranging 1920
> marbling 1958

−ish. Forming adjectives, usually meaning 'of the character of' or 'tending to':

> blondish 1961
> folklorish 1926
> gangsterish 1945
> humpish 1936
> leftish 1934

−ism. Among the commonest uses of this suffix are: (1) forming words to express the action or conduct of a class of persons or the condition of a person or thing; (2) forming the name of religious, philosophical, political, etc systems of theory or practice, and also descriptive terms for doctrines or principles; (3) forming terms denoting a peculiarity or characteristic, especially of language:

automatonism 1925
developmentalism 1934
fundamentalism 1923
gangsterism 1927
Goldwaterism (rigid conservatism, as represented by
    the views and policies of the American
    Republican politician, Barry Goldwater) 1960
isolationism 1922
Leftism 1920
McCarthyism (the policy of hunting out [suspected]
    Communists – from the name of the American
    senator Joseph McCarthy) 1950
Naderism (public agitation for greater safety and
    higher quality of consumer goods – from the name
    of the American lawyer, Ralph Nader) 1969

−*ist*. Forming agent nouns, nouns designating a person who practises or follows some art or method, nouns designating adherents to some doctrine or system, etc. Many of these can also be used adjectivally:

assimilationist (one who advocates the integration of
    different races, cultural groups, etc) 1928
aversionist 1938
escapist 1930
fantasist 1923
fundamentalist 1922

−*istic*. Forming adjectives:

narcissistic 1916

−*ite*. Forming adjectives and nouns with the sense '(one) connected with or belonging to'. Also used freely in the

Head lights.

formation of the names of minerals and some organic compounds:

> englishite (a mineral) 1930
> Hitlerite 1930
> Nasserite (a supporter of the Egyptian President
>   Gamel Abdel Nasser) 1958

−*itis*. Used to form names of inflammatory diseases, and also in trivial use:

> electionitis 1945
> localitis (colloquial name for undue concern with a
>   small area of the world) 1943

−ive. Forming adjectives (which can often be used as nouns) with the sense 'lending to, having the nature of':

> appraisive 1934
> assaultive 1955
> benefactive 1943
> exploitive 1921
> impactive 1934

−ization. Forming nouns of action:

> Egyptianization 1957
> ghettoization 1939
> gregarization (the swarming of locusts) 1939
> lyophilization (freeze-drying) 1938
> nativization 1940

−ize. A common verbal suffix:

> absolutize 1936
> accessorize 1939
> anthropologize 1939
> fantasize 1926
> ghettoize 1939
> glamorize 1936
> nativize 1933

−kin. A diminutive suffix:

> lovekin 1922

−less. Forming adjectives, meaning 'without':

> endingless 1946
> flapless 1916
> flareless 1932
> gimmickless 1962
> Hunless 1920
> kinkless 1943

−*let*. A diminutive suffix:

boblet (a bob-sleigh for two persons) 1914
filmlet 1931
flatlet 1925

−*ly*. 1 Forming adjectives with the sense 'having the qualities of':

leaderly 1918
modelly 1961

2 Forming adverbs, mainly from adjectives:

banally 1934
behaviourally 1936
berserkly 1963
bitchily 1938
evolutionarily 1945
globally 1930
glueily 1925
impractically 1947
logistically 1932
matily 1973

−*mane*. Forming nouns meaning 'one who has a mania for (something)':

balletomane (an enthusiast for ballet performances) 1930

−*mania*. Denoting a craze for (something):

Beatlemania (the pop group 'The Beatles') 1963
hippomania (excessive fondness for horses) 1961
islomania (a passion for islands) 1962

−*manship*. Used to denote skill in a subject or activity, now especially deployed in such a way as to disconcert a rival or opponent. This traditional terminal element underwent a profound change of meaning in 1947 under the influence of *gamesmanship*, introduced in Stephen Potter's book *The Theory & Practice of Gamesmanship or The Art of Winning Games Without ActuallyCheating*:

brinkmanship (the art of advancing to the very brink of
    war but not engaging in it) 1956
conferencemanship 1962
do-it-yourself-manship 1955
lifemanship (skill in getting the edge over, or acquiring
    an advantage over, another person or persons –
    also introduced by Stephen Potter) 1950
namesmanship (skill in name-dropping) 1964
queuemanship 1950

−*mat*. A modern suffix denoting devices that work automatically or a business that contains automatic or self-service equipment. Many of these words are proprietary terms:

Laundromat 1943
Mail-O-Mat 1951
Nickel-mat 1935

−*mere*. Used in biological terms with the sense 'part', 'segment':

centromere 1935
genomere 1928

−*ness*. Used to form nouns of state or condition, usually from adjectives:

> averageness 1925
> bogusness 1921
> browned-offness 1943
> depressingness 1923
> emotionlessness 1921
> frowstiness 1923
> go-gettingness 1926
> goofiness 1929
> goshawfulness 1934
> kinkiness 1924
> middle-classness 1923
> nanniness 1973

−*nik*. Another recent suffix, derived from Russian and Yiddish, and forming nouns denoting a person or thing involved in or associated with the things or quality specified:

> beatnik 1958
> computernik 1966
> draftnik 1965
> folknik 1958
> neatnik 1959
> no-goodnik 1960
> protestnik 1965
> Vietnik 1965

−*o*. A slang or colloquial ending, chiefly used in Australia and New Zealand, and often attached to the shortened forms of words:

> ammo (ammunition) 1917
> Fatso (nickname for a fat person) 1944
> garbo (Australian slang for a dustman) 1953
> Nasho (Australian slang for a national service(man)
>   1962

−*ocracy*. Denoting the rule of any class:

    meritocracy 1958

−*oid*. Forming adjectives and nouns, and meaning '(something) having the form or nature of, resembling, allied to':

    feminoid 1923
    gorilloid 1946
    humanoid 1918
    liberaloid 1951
    masculinoid 1921

−*ologist*. Denoting one who specializes in a particular art or science:

    escapologist 1926
    garbologist (a dustman) 1965

−*ology*. Forming the names of arts or sciences:

    anaesthesiology 1914
    futurology 1946
    hormonology 1918

−*or*. Forming (usually agent) nouns:

    attenuator 1924
    inactivator 1944
    laminator 1941

−*ory*. Forming adjectives, usually with reference to a verbal action:

identificatory 1943

−*osis*. Often used in the names of diseases or medical conditions:

asbestosis (a lung disease caused by inhaling asbestos
    particles) 1927
brucellosis 1930

−*ous*. Forming adjectives meaning 'full of', 'characterized by' etc:

beatitudinous 1926

−*phil(e)*. Signifying a lover or adherent of something:

gerontophil (of old people) 1918
gramophile (of the gramophone or gramophone
    records) 1922
jazzophile 1941
leprophil (of sufferers from leprosy) 1959

−*philia*. Signifying love of something:

neophilia (love of novelty) 1932

phobia. Signifying fear of something:

logophobia (fear of words) 1923

—plasty. Meaning 'moulding, formation', and used in terms of surgery:

isoplasty (transplanting tissue) 1923
mammoplasty (plastic surgery on the breast) 1938

—scope. Forming names of scientific instruments or contrivances for enabling the eye to view or examine:

anomaloscope (for measuring abnormality in volour
          vision) 1923
fibrescope (for viewing inaccessible passages in the
          body, etc) 1954
gonioscope (for observing part of the eye) 1925

—some (1) Forming adjectives meaning 'characterized by being':

grumblesome 1925
knucklesome 1919

(2) Used in biology, denoting a portion of a body,
          especially a cell:

episome 1931
lysosome 1955

—ster. Used frequently in trade-designations, or in suggesting a way of life, occasionally derogatory, but also with other functions:

beatster (one of the 'beat' generation) 1959
dragster (a hot-rod) car 1954
gagster (a gag-writer or comedian) 1935
hepster (a 'hep-cat', one fond of jazz or swing etc)
    1938
kickster (one who lives 'for kicks') 1963
mobster 1917

−*tomy*. Used in surgical terms and indicating 'cutting':

lobotomy (incision into a lobe, especially into the
    frontal lobe of the brain) 1936

−*ward(s)*. Forming adverbs meaning 'in the direction of';
etc:

longwards 1971
loveward(s) 1927

−*y*. Numerous suffixes have this form:

(1) Forming adjectives with the general sense 'having
    the qualities of, full of':

autumny 1916
beaty 1956
busty 1944
fiddly 1926
gimmicky 1957
goofy 1921
iffy (uncertain, doubtful) 1937

(2) Forming abstract nouns of quality or condition:

isometry 1941

(3) With the common variant −*ie*, forming pet names and familiar diminutives:

> baddy 1937
> biggie 1937
> falsies (padded breasts) 1943
> hippie 1953
> hotty, −ie (a hot-water bottle) 1947
> junkie 1923
> meany 1927
> Nessie (familiar name for the 'Loch Ness Monster') 1945

The second additive process of word formation involves prefixes or special combining forms. The semantic rather than the grammatical (changing part of speech, etc) element is more important in prefixes than in suffixes. I won't take such a close look at prefixes as I did at suffixes, since new words can be found together in an alphabetical cluster in dictionaries whereas you would need a reverse dictionary to find together all those words formed with the same suffix. Instead we shall just look at some prefixes, beginning with one of two letters, *m* and *n*, in the hope that they will give you an idea of the large numbers of these formative elements in English.

macro−. Meaning long, large, comprehensive, etc, and common in scientific terms:

> macroanalysis 1938
> macroclimate 1939
> macro-economics 1948

magico−. The combining form of *magical* with other adjectives:

> magico-oriental 1930
> magico-religious 1941

magneto—. Denoting processes carried on by magnetic means, or the application of magnetism to particular departments of art or industry:

> magnetohydrodynamics 1950
> magnetopause 1963
> magnetosphere 1959

mal—. Meaning ill, wrong, or improper(ly):

> malabsorption 1932
> malfunction 1928
> malnourishment 1932

matri—. Meaning 'mother', and used in anthropology and sociology in various words denoting aspects of social organization defined by relationship through women:

> matricentred 1956
> matriclan 1950
> matrifocal 1952

maxi—. Denoting things, especially articles of clothing, which are very long or large of their kind. A very recent prefix:

> maxi-bag 1966
> maxi-budget 1975
> maxi-coat 1968

mechano—. In the sense 'mechanical and something else':

> mechanochemistry 1928
> mechanoelectric 1958
> mechanoelectrical 1961

mega–. In many (especially scientific) terms, meaning 'very large':

    megacity (a very large city) 1968
    megacorpse (a million dead bodies – used in estimating
        the possible effects of nuclear warfare) 1958
    megamillionaire 1968

Brain Storm..

meta—. In one of its uses, prefixed to the name of a science to form a designation of a higher science (actual or hypothetical) of the same nature but dealing with problems of an ulterior or more fundamental nature:

> metabiology (a term introduced by George Bernard
>   Shaw in *Back to Methuselah*) 1921
> metaethics 1949
> metahistory 1957

micro—. This prefix has too many uses for complete enumeration, but two recent extensions of its domain are:

> (1) to denote extreme shortness of a woman's
>   garment:

> micromini (a very short miniskirt) 1967

> (2) indicating that the object designated has been
>   reduced in size by the use of microphotography,
>   or is used in connection with such an object:

> microbook 1970
> microfiche 1950
> microfilm 1935

midi—. A new prefix used in the language of fashion, and denoting garments longer than mini— but shorter than maxi—, usually extending to mid-calf:

> midi-coat 1968
> midi-dress 1970
> midi-skirt 1967

milli—. Denoting the thousandth part of a metric unit:

> milli-degree 1951
> milli-watt 1929

mini—. Used to designate things that are very small of their kind, and very much in vogue in the 1960s:

    mini-bag 1966
    mini-budget 1966
    mini-computer 1968
    minicab 1960
    minifarm 1969
    minimarathon 1972
    minipill 1970
    mini-skirt 1965

mis—. 'Bad or imperfect':

    misalignment 1924
    misallocation 1950
    misdial (vb.) 1964
    mislabelling 1952

mono—. Signifying 'only, sole, single', etc:

    monoculture 1915
    monokini (after bikini) 1964
    monosexual 1964

multi—. Signifying 'many', usually with adjectives or nouns used attributively:

    multicultural 1941
    multifunctional 1941
    multi-level 1952
    multinational 1926
    multi-purpose 1935
    multi-racial 1923
    multi-storey 1918
    multiversity (a very large university) 1963

nano—. A modern scientific prefix. With the names of units, forming the names of units which are a one thousand-millionth part of them:

    nanocamp 1973
    nanogram 1951
    nanosecond 1959

neo—. 'New':

    neo-Fascism 1946
    neoglacial 1960
    neoglaciation 1951
    neonate (a new-born infant) 1932
    neo-populism 1972
    neo-Victorian 1929

neuro—. Pertaining to the nervous system:

    neurochemistry 1955
    neuropsychiatry 1918
    neurosurgeon 1925

non—. This prefix has continued to be one of the great formative elements in English. It would be impossible to list here even a fraction of the new words formed by using it. However, a new use can be mentioned: where *non—* is prefixed to a noun with an implication of pretence, to denote someone or something not really what is specified by the noun. It is used especially of forms of art and literature, and often implies that they are new or unconventional forms of the things specified:

    non-answer 1966
    non-architecture 1960
    non-book 1960
    non-Budget 1967
    non-debate 1970

non-event 1962
non-film 1963
non-hero 1940
non-music 1958

normo—. Used in biological and medical words, especially in physiology, to express the condition of being close to the average in respect of any particular character that varies:

normochromic 1935
normolensive 1941

Combining two words is the third additive method of word formation to look at. In forming nouns in particular, the point at which two words in juxtaposition can be regarded as one inseparable word is often hard to determine, and in the early stages of a word's history the elements are often written separately. When there is a close syntactic relationship between the parts, however (as in the verb-object relation in *brainwashing*), or when the new word is used as a verb or adjective, the status of the formation is easier to determine. Here are some examples:

backdate (vb) 1946
brainwashing 1950
gate-crasher 1927
go-slow 1930
grant-aided 1927
hair-do 1932
layabout 1932
lookalike (noun) 1947
machine-wash 1960
newsworthy 1932
nitpicker 1951
nohoper 1943

Verb and particle or adverb constructions often form nouns or adjectives. For example:

been-to (a term used in Africa and Asia for a person
     who has been to England, usually for education)
     1960
blast-off 1951
brown-out (a partial black-out) 1942
bunk-up 1919
fade-out 1918
fall-out 1950
fly-by 1953
fly-past 1914
freak-out 1966
fry-up 1967
gang-up 1936
iron-on (adj) 1959
layup 1927
laze-off 1924
lead-up 1953
link-up 1945
live-in (adj) 1955
mark-up 1920

Two more words can also be *blended* to form a new word: for
example, *breathalyser* (breath + analyser), 1960, and *identi-
kit* (identity + kit), 1961.

As well as forming new words by building-up, you can
create them by subtraction and shortening. A word formed by
removing a suffix or prefix is known as a 'back-formation'.
Recent examples include:

auto-suggest (vb from auto-suggestion, 1890) 1921
back-stab (vb from back-stabber, 1906) 1925
brainwash (vb from brain-washing, 1950) 1953
escalate (vb from escalator, 1900) 1922
fluoridate (vb from fluoridation, 1904) 1949
gold-dig (vb from gold-digger in the sense of a girl or
     woman who attaches herself to a man merely for
     gain, 1920) 1926
gruntled (adj from disgruntled, nineteenth century)
     P G Wodehouse, 1938

liaise (from liaison, seventeenth century) 1928
loud-hail (vb from loud-hailer, 1941) 1943

New words are also frequently created by shortening old ones, and occasionally also adding a suffix such as *ie−* or *−o* to the resulting form. This is particularly common in slang and colloquial English, especially in military slang, though it is by no means restricted to these areas. Here are some examples:

admin (administration) 1942
bio (biography) 1961
biog (biography) 1942
blitz (Blitzkrieg, German) 1940
bot (bottom) 1922
fratting (fraternizing) 1945
glad (from gladiolus) 1923
glam (glamorous) 1936
grot (grotesque, in typography) 1961
gump (gumption) 1920
hash (hashish) 1959
hetero (heterosexual) 1933
hype (hypodermic) 1924
lib (liberation) 1970
libber (liberationist) 1971
limo (limousine) 1968
Med (Mediterranean) 1948
met (meteorological office[r]) 1940
mike (microgram) 1970
mini (mini-car, -cab) 1961
mod (modern – a type of teenager, contrasted with
    rocker) 1960
mog (moggy, a cat) 1927
narc (narcotic – a narcotics agent) 1967
natch (naturally) 1945
Nes (Nescafé) 1968
nuke (nuclear-bomb, weapon, etc) 1959
nympho (nymphomaniac) 1935

We now venture into the less reputable area of acronyms and initialisms. These have become so numerous that specialized dictionaries treating them have been published and can be consulted for examples. I will only list a very few here:

Amgot, *A*llied *M*ilitary *G*overnment of *O*ccupied *T*erritory, the title of an organization first set up in Sicily during World War II, 1943.
Anzac, from *A*ustralian and *N*ew *Z*ealand *A*rmy *C*orps, and used colloquially for a member of that corps, or for any Australian or New Zealand serviceman, 1915.
laser, from *l*ight *a*mplification by the *s*timulated *e*mission of radiation, 1960.
Nibmar, from *n*o *i*ndependence *b*efore *m*ajority *A*frican *r*ule, the policy of opposing recognition of the minority government which proclaimed the independence of Rhodesia in 1965, 1966.
notam, from *no*tice to *a*ir*m*en, a warning notice to pilots, 1946.

New discoveries and inventions demand a high degree of linguistic creativity from scientists, and they have responded to the challenge with ingenuity if without much regard for the history and traditions of English. Look at a few examples of the new scientific terminology beginning with the letter *n*:

nabam, from *Na*, the chemical symbol for sodium and bis-dithiocar*bam*ate, a water-soluble powder used as a fungicide, 1950.
nahcolite, from $NaHCO_3$, its chemical formula, and the suffix −*lite* − sodium bicarbonate, 1928.
napalm, a blend of *na*phthenate and *palm*itate, 1942.
nekoite, an anagram of *okenite*, and a form of calcium silicate, 1956.
Nitinol, from *Ni*, the chemical symbol for nickel, *Ti*, the chemical symbol for titanium, and the initial letters of *N*aval *O*rdinance *L*aboratory, Silver Spring, Maryland, USA, the place of work of the metallurgists who discovered the alloy and invented its name − an alloy of nickel and titanium, 1968.

*

Proprietary terms are another area where there is scope for linguistic invention. A brand name may follow established modes of word formation, be an arbitrary creation, or merely involve a modification of spelling. One of the most successful and best-known is 'nylon' (1938). Derivations for this word are frequently given, but none is supported by evidence. In fact, a representative of the du Pont company, which developed substances known as 'nylon', has emphasized that 'The letters n-y-l-o-n have absolutely no significance,

Beauty Spot..

etymological or otherwise. Because the names of two textile fibres in common use – namely "cotton" and "rayon", end with the letters "on" it was felt that a word ending in "on" might be desirable. A number of words were rejected because it was found that they were not sufficiently distinct from words found in the dictionary, or in lists of classified trademarks. After much deliberation, the term "nylon" was finally adopted.'

I have not explored *all* the resources for creating new English vocabulary, but I think I have touched on the most common, so now, if you are ever confronted by a situation requiring a term for a novel idea or a new object, I trust you will have no difficulty in coining an apt and telling word.

Wayward Words

'Hey ho,' the chaplain sighed, 'such are the vicissitudes of this our sublunary experience.' I looked uncomprehending. He looked gratified and condescendingly obliged with a translation. 'Such is life.'

And so indeed it is.

We live in a world where verbal diarrhoea has reached epidemic proportions, a world where the airline hostess tells you 'there is some precipitation' when she means 'it's raining'; where the boss asks you 'to work with unusually distant time-horizons', when he wants you to plan ahead; where the architect declares that 'long passages have visual unattractiveness' when he means that long passages are ugly; and where bright young men like the chaplain I knew at Oxford tell you 'a slight inclination of the cranium is as adequate as a spasmodic movement of one optic to an equine quadruped utterly devoid of any visionary capacity', when they simply mean to say 'a nod's as good as a wink to a blind horse'.

No stratum of civilized society has escaped infection. People from all walks of life appear increasingly unable to resist the temptation to use two or three or, better still, four words where one would do. The simple is eschewed in favour of the complex, the monosyllabic in favour of the polysyllabic, the easily comprehensible in favour of the almost incomprehensible.

Sir Bruce Fraser in his revised edition of Sir Ernest Gowers' magisterial work, *The Complete Plain Words* 'gives a number' of mind-boggling examples of contemporary gobbledygook. Just feast your eyes on these two passages, written to be read by 'ordinary students' of business and personnel management:

The cognitive continuum is concerned with objectives related to knowledge and the intellectual abilities and skills, rising from comprehension to evaluation. The effective continuum covers the range of behavioural responses, from passive acceptance of stimuli to the organisation of taught values into a complex system which constitutes the whole characterisation of an individual.

In the second place there are grounds for thinking that the availability of analytical assessments of jobs would facilitate the preparation of grade-descriptions for a new structure in a situation in which the allocation of jobs to grades at the stages of implementing and maintaining that structure would be undertaken by whole-job procedures.

If ever you have wondered why doctors cultivate illegible handwriting, could it be that they are determined to deny you the pleasure of reading a gem like this?

Experiments are described which demonstrate that in normal individuals the lowest concentration in which sucrose can be detected by means of gustation differs from the lowest concentration in which sucrose (in the amount employed) has to be ingested in order to produce a demonstrable decrease in olfactory acuity and a noteworthy conversion of sensations interpreted as a desire for food into sensations interpreted as a satiety associated with ingestion of food.

All he is trying to say, believe it or not, is that experiments show that a normal person can taste sugar in water in quantities not strong enough to interfere with his sense of smell or take away his appetite!

What is sad is that those most often guilty of arcane rubbish like this are those from whom you might least expect it: doctors, scientists, lawyers, academics, people the nature of whose calling requires at least a theoretical mental discipline and a clarity and economy of expression. Those who have always felt that sociology was a pseudo-science will not be surprised to learn that 'a set of arrangements for producing and rearing children the viability of which is not predicated on the consistent presence in the household of an adult male acting in the role of husband and father', is one American sociologist's way of saying, 'dad isn't home much', but it will sadden anyone with any faith left in the ability of 'professional training' actually to train anyone for a profession.

Sir Winston Churchill, a true master of the English language, loathed verbiage and deplored its increasing prevalence. On 9 August 1940, shortly after the signing of the French armistice and the occupation of the Channel Islands, when the Battle of Britain was raging overhead, he found time to write a memorandum called 'Brevity':

Let us have an end to such phrases as these: 'It is also of importance to bear in mind the following considerations . . .' or 'consideration should be given to the possibility of carrying into effect . . .' Most of these woolly phrases are mere padding, which can be left out altogether, or replaced by a single word. Let us not shrink from using the short expressive phrase even if it is conversational.

Lord Palmerston, who was Prime Minister almost a century before Churchill, felt the same way. He issued instructions to all of 'Her Majesty's Ministers abroad' to go through their despatches striking out any words not necessary for fully conveying their meaning. One such Minister, a Mr Hamilton, failed to follow the instruction. Palmerston sent him a lordly rebuke: 'If Mr Hamilton would let his substantives and adjectives go single instead of always sending them forth by twos and threes, his despatches would be clearer and easier to read.'

Using two words where one would do is always unnecessary. Often it is technically inaccurate as well. 'Tautology' is a repetition of the same statement, and I know of no one who isn't guilty of the occasional tautological utterance. If you think this is one area where you may be an innocent, glance through the next few sentences and make sure you have never committed any of the tautologies they contain.

I think ten bottles will be adequate enough for the party.
The carbon copy is attached hereto.
When you have finished with the secret file I would be
    grateful if you would be sure to burn it up.
If we continue to collaborate together I'm sure all will go
    well.
This is an issue I want to debate about.
Let's descend down to the rumpus room.
I am looking forward to the final completion of the
    project.
When we first began to make love you were more
    enthusiastic.
I will be following after you.
I would be grateful if you could forbear from smoking
    while you are feeding the baby.
You shouldn't have laughed at your own mother's
    funeral obsequies.
I hope you won't forget all the important essentials.
I'll put the cheque inside of the envelope right away.
This joint cooperation should prove rewarding.
I weigh just exactly 10 stone.
Let's meet together next summer.
He is more superior to you.
Mutual cooperation is essential if we are to succeed.
I'm a new beginner so I hope you'll help me.
Thank God 1988 is nearly over with!
What a pretty pair of twins.
The failure of my marriage is past history.
Are you planning to penetrate into the jungle?
Is there anything you would like me to repeat again?
I hope we can still remain friends.
I would like to taste of the rhubarb wine.
Let us unite together this man and this woman.
She was a sad-looking widow woman.
The aircraft was circling round over Chicago.
That will leave me with twenty apples left.

There you have 30 sentences with a superfluous word in each.
To turn them into correct English, all you need do is cross out
enough, hereto, up, together, about, down, final, first, after,

from, obsequies, important, of, joint, just, together, more, mutual, new, with, a pair, past, into, again, still, of, together, woman, round and left. Tautology is ugly and ignorant and a waste of breath.

I say this so sweepingly, yet I know that my own conversation is peppered with unnecessary words. 'You know,' 'I mean', 'sort of', 'like er –' are phrases that do no work and get in the way of what I am trying to say. 'You know, I'm feeling sort of tired like and, er, I think I'll sort of go to bed, if you know what I mean,' is not the clearest way of saying I don't want to go out tonight.

Sometimes, of course, these superfluous phrases do serve a purpose. They can provide useful thinking time. They can be used for emphasis. ('What was Julie like?' 'Julie who?' 'Julie, *you know*.' 'Oh, that Julie? She was pathetic, *I mean*, pathetic.') They can be used to lessen the impact of an unpleasant truth. ('I am, I mean, a lot younger than you.') They can be used to indicate a certain becoming hesitancy and sense of discretion. ('She's, you know, permanently drunk.' 'He's become, like, raving mad.' 'She is a sort of nymphomaniac, actually.')

On the whole, however, these bits of linguistic flotsam serve no purpose and yet every day they seem to become a more prominent part of our vocabulary. From the mouths of many (myself included) a sentence would now seem incomplete if it didn't contain a fair sprinkling of junk phrases.

In 1858, the American writer, Oliver Wendell Holmes, coined the word *verbicide*. He used it to describe the 'violent treatment of a word with fatal results to its legitimate meaning, which is its life.' Here are some recent victims of verbicide:

amazing	ghastly
awful	hectic
awfully	horrible
beastly	incredible
deadly	livid
definitely	literally
dreadful	marvellous
fantastic	manic
fabulous	nostalgia

frightful	phenomenal
fearsome	simply
fearful	shocking
frantic	stupendous
fiendish	terrible
great	terrific
gorgeous	weird
gigantic	wonderful

I picked those words at random. You could draw up your own list of words that have been battered to death through excessive and thoughtless use. Some are vogue words (viable, chauvinist, potential, feasible, increment, cholesterol) that enjoy a brief mayfly glory during which they are on everybody's lips. Others are more humdrum words (nice, great, super) that have been used so often and so indiscriminately that they have lost all their cutting edge.

In the entertainment industry verbicide is a way of life. I have heard failures described as 'hits' and moderate successes hailed as 'smasheroos'. We take it for granted that 'the special guest star' is neither special, nor a star and appears every week. Because a TV actor of whom hardly anybody has ever heard is described as a 'star', the real stars have to be described as 'zonking great super superstars'. When Sam Goldwyn was asked how business was, he replied as only a king of the movies could, 'Colossal but it's improving.' When the remake of *King Kong* was screened in 1976 it was billed as 'the most original motion picture of all time'.

There are adjectives that are incomparable, absolute, unmodifiable – complete, contemporary, everlasting, indestructible, meaningless, omnipotent, perfect, supreme, for example – but that doesn't seem to stop people from trying to modify them, describing this cook-book as more complete than that, this novel as more contemporary than that, this taste as more perfectly perfect than that. As words become devalued we have to bolster them up with other words. Now that 'a disaster' on its own doesn't sound too awful, we have to talk about 'a terrible disaster'. Since 'a terrible disaster' doesn't sound quite as dreadful as it did, we have to call it 'a truly terrible disaster'. Eventually it becomes 'a truly incredibly terrible disaster of catastrophic proportions' and it still doesn't move us much. When you see one word on a page printed in *italics*, you know the italics are adding emphasis to that word. When a whole book is printed in italics, you pay no attention to them.

Ernest Bevin, Britain's Foreign Secretary in the years immediately following the Second World War, once complained of Aneurin Bevan, architect of Britain's National Health Service, 'All 'e ever says is clitch, clitch, clitch, clitch.' If you listen to the conversation of many people today all you seem to hear is cliché after cliché after cliché, and as often as not these overworked phrases are strung together with overworked words. Clichés are spoken without thought. That is the essence of them; they don't need to be considered, they just come tumbling out automatically. It doesn't matter to the users how hackneyed they are: their very familiarity is reassuring. It doesn't matter that they are often imprecise and inappropriate: they convey a gist of a meaning and for most purposes that is good enough. In conversation, many people are unsure of themselves and want to be 'on safe ground';

they like to show the people they are addressing that they 'belong'. When people swap clichés it signals that they are speaking the same language on the same terms.

Many clichés express thoughts economically and imaginatively. Or rather they did once upon a time, years ago, when they were new-minted. 'He's at death's door', 'don't beat about the bush', 'feel as free as air', 'the long arm of coincidence', were once fresh and telling phrases. They weren't clichés then, but much as we might like to 'put the clock back', it isn't possible. Once a phrase becomes a cliché it remains a cliché. To use tomorrow's clichés today is to be inventive and original. To use today's clichés today is to be linguistically lazy and uncreatively conventional.

Slang isn't always conventional, but it is often a sign of laziness, an easy shorthand that requires no mental energy. American poet, Carl Sandburg, said, 'Slang is a language that rolls up its sleeves, spits on its hands and goes to work,' but that is perhaps a sentimental view that a poet of Sandburg's calibre could afford. He was able to use the raw material of local idiom, folk language and slang with rare creative force. A man who can describe poetry as 'the achievement of the synthesis of hyacinths and biscuits' is the sort of man who *can* create clichés for tomorrow: he is an original who doesn't fall back on slang because he can't be bothered to think of anything more worthwhile; he goes for the slang because he knows how to use it. The rest of us aren't so fortunate.

'Words', according to another master of them, Joseph Conrad, 'are the great foes of reality.' They need not be, but they have become so, most often perhaps in the mouths of politicians. When in 1956, the Prime Minister, Sir Anthony Eden, declared in parliament: 'We are not at war with Egypt: we are in a state of armed conflict,' there were many who knew the truth behind this risible statement, but there were many more who did not. Just as there are those who still believe that 'if it's in print' it *must* be true, there were then those who believed that the words of the Queen's First Minister, spoken in the Mother of Parliaments, *must* be accepted at face value. Of course, in terms of semantic gymnastics, Sir Anthony Eden was an innocent compared with the United States Pentagon, according to whom, for example, the Vietnam War was not war at all – it was 'international armed conflict'; the bombardment of defenceless villages was 'pacification', the migration of thousands of homeless peasants was a 'transfer of population' and their refugee camps weren't really refugee camps: they were 'new life hamlets'! 'A routine limited duration protective reaction' was the phrase used to disguise the lethal reality of a major air raid, and when the bombs fell on friendly villages the mistakes were termed 'navigation misdirections'. The defoliation of entire forests was just part of a 'resources control program,' the use of napalm was simply one aspect of a 'momentary defensive strategy,' and the thirty-four dollars given to the families of South Vietnamese civilians killed in error were generously called 'condolence awards'.

Naturally, during the Vietnam War the other side were playing the same game. At the time writer, Roy Colby, drew up a list of some of the 'Communese' turns of phrase that emanated from Hanoi and provided his own translations:

patriotic, pro-Communist
compatriot, fellow-Communist
heroic acts, treasonable crimes
monstrous crimes, U.S. military successes
provocation, defensive steps
build a free and happy life, undergo Communist
    regimentation
mankind, international Communism
liberate, conquer
progressive, following the Communist party line
democratic regime, Communist colonialism
landlords, landowners
land reform, confiscation
pressgang mercenaries, US troops

George Orwell recognized how, in our time, political speech and writing are largely devoted to 'the defence of the indefensible'. In his essay 'Politics and the English Language', written in 1946, he conjured up a picture of 'some comfortable English professor defending Russian totalitarianism. He cannot say outright, "I believe in killing off your opponents when you can get good results by doing so." Probably, therefore, he will say something like this: "While freely conceding that the Soviet regime exhibits certain features which the humanitarian may be inclined to deplore, we must, I think, agree that a certain curtailment of the rights to political opposition is an unavoidable concomitant of transitional periods, and that the rigours which the Russian people have been called upon to undergo have been amply justified in the sphere of concrete achievement."'

In Orwell's prophetic novel *1984* (which was published in 1949 and which Orwell had wanted to call *1948*), the country was controlled by four Ministries whose very names belied their roles: Minipax, the Ministry of Peace dealt with war, Minitrue, the Ministry of Truth dealt with propaganda, Miniluv, the Ministry of Love dealt with law and order, and the Ministry of Plenty dealt with scarcities. The language of *1984* was 'Newspeak' which contained a special vocabulary of words constructed for political purposes, intended not only to deceive the hearer and reader, but also to 'impose a desirable mental attitude upon the person using them'. It all sounds a bit far-fetched until you visit modern South Africa and come face to face with officially 'single' people who are actually married but cannot live with their families because their colours don't match. Apartheid is 'separate development'. The 'Extension of University Education Act' prevents mixed-race universities. The 'Prohibition of Political Interference Act' forbids racially mixed political parties. The South African government's linguistic 'defence of the indefensible' is as Orwellian as anything you will find in *1984*.

Evasion of the truth by the ingenious use of language is not a new weapon in the politician's armoury. Benjamin Disraeli, a favourite Prime Minister of Queen Victoria, was an adept user of words to his own advantage. In his novel *Coningsby* he lifted the veil for a moment when two of his characters were discussing their party's battle cry for the forthcoming election:

'And now for our cry,' said Mr Taper.
'It is not a Cabinet for a good cry,' said Tadpole; 'but them, on the other hand, it is a Cabinet that will sow

dissension on the opposite ranks, and prevent them having a good cry.'

'Ancient institutions and modern improvements, I suppose, Mr Tadpole.'

'Ameliorations is the better word; ameliorations. Nobody knows exactly what it means.'

For all our cynical distrust of the deceptive language of the politician, we contrive unconsciously to deceive ourselves all the time. Our everyday vocabulary includes examples of pretension of every kind – ostentatious words, affected words, foreign words, archaic words – designed to impress and so intended, albeit innocently, to deceive.

In Dickens's *David Copperfield*, Mr Micawber, whose capacity for self-deception knows few bounds, has the endearing knack of following a flow of verbal pomposities with a more humble explanation of what he has just said: '"Under the impression," said Mr Micawber, "that your peregrinations in the metropolis have not yet been extensive, and that you might have some difficulty in penetrating the arcana of the Modern Babylon . . . in short," said Mr Micawber in a burst of confidence, "that you might lose your way . . ."' Most of us don't trouble to translate our pretentious effusions; unless we take the precaution of putting them in inverted commas as we speak, so alerting our listeners to the fact that we are saying something we inwardly know we are not at home with but that we hope to get away with none the less, we speak pretentiously as though 'to the manner born' and naively trust that our listeners will do as we do and mistake the grandiose for the grand.

While recognizing euphuism ('an artificial or affected style'), we probably reckon that it's a pretension of which we are only occasionally to be found guilty. The same cannot be said for euphemism ('the substitution of a mild or vague expression for a harsh or blunt one'), an instinct as old as language itself and one to which we all give in more frequently than we realize. The Greek historian, Plutarch, writing in the first century AD about life in the sixth century BC, recorded that 'the Ancient Athenians used to cover up the ugliness of things with auspicious and kindly terms, giving them polite and endearing names. Thus they called harlots "compan-ions", taxes "contributions", and the prison a "chamber".'

To the genteel of only a generation or two ago a bitch was always 'a lady dog', and a bull a 'he-cow' or a 'gentleman cow' or a 'male beast' or a 'critter' or a 'sire' or a 'brute' or 'the big animal' or *anything* save a 'bull'. And can you guess the nature of the garment that a century ago could have been described as 'irrepressibles', 'indescribables', 'ineffables', 'inexpressibles', 'unutterables', 'indispensables', 'innomina-bles', 'inexplicables', 'unwhisperables' and 'unmentiona-bles'? Well, you are not wrong. They were not *originally* euphemisms for underpants. They were euphemisms for ordi-nary trousers! What went into those 'unmentionables' (which were trousers for the early Victorians but, more daringly, underpants for the late Victorians) were 'benders', 'under-standings', 'underpinners', 'extremities' or even—wait for it—'crural appendages'. The Victorian piano didn't have legs; it was supported on 'limbs'.

There are those who believe that all euphemisms are wrong because all euphemisms represent an element of self-deception. I don't agree. If there are times and places when it would be kinder, more courteous, less hurtful and less embar-rassing to use a euphemism, why not be kind and courteous and save others from needless hurt and embarrassment? The euphemisms I do deplore are the ones that lull us into a false sense of security and help us fool ourselves about the realities of life that we ought not to be avoiding. Does talking about 'correctional therapeutic communities', 'clinics for the emo-tionally disadvantaged', and the problems of the 'socially disadvantaged underachievers' really help us get to grips with what we ought to be doing with our prisons, mental hospitals, and backward children from poor backgrounds? In America today a window-cleaner is 'a glass maintenance engineer', a chimney sweep is a 'scandiscopist', a gardener is a 'landscape technician', a tax collector is a 'revenue agent', a barber is a 'hair stylist', a film projectionist is a 'multimedia systems technician', a dog catcher is a 'canine control officer', a filing clerk is an 'information retrieval administrator', a janitor is a 'sanitation maintenance superintendent' and a dirty old man is a 'sexy senior citizen'. These are euphemisms that only flirt

with the truth and, with the exception of the last example, add
nothing to the dignity of the occupations they describe.

I suppose that anyone interested enough in words to be
reading this book will already be doing their best to avoid
gobbledygook, tautology, junk words, jargon, clichés, euphemisms and euphuisms. If you're trying and not quite
succeeding you might like a set of Rules for Writing Good
English. You will find such rules set out at length in such
classics as *The Complete Plain Words* – from which I have
borrowed many of the entertaining examples of *bad* English
quoted above – and H W and F G Fowler's *The King's English*
but for concise advice, and for rules that can be quickly
assimilated and not easily forgotten, I think it would be
difficult to better the six offered by George Orwell in 1946:

1 Never use a metaphor, simile or other figure of speech
   which you are used to seeing in print.
2 Never use a long word where a short one will do.
3 If it is possible to cut a word out, always cut it out.

Leg before Wicket.

4 Never use the passive where you can use the active.
5 Never use a foreign phrase, a scientific word or a jargon word if you can think of an everyday English equivalent.
6 Break any of these rules sooner than say anything outright barbarous.

Follow those rules and your writing may not be as good as Orwell's, but it will at least be easy to read and easy to understand. What's more, as Orwell noted, 'when you make a stupid remark its stupidity will be obvious, even to yourself'.

PART TWO

WORD PLAY

Introduction

In writing about the history of words and the uses and abuses to which they have been subjected, I have done my best to underline the fact that I love words so much because they're such *fun*. And that's why I'm devoting the rest of the book to a rag-bag of my favourite word 'entertainments', games and puzzles. Some may turn out to be rather more sophisticated than you'd expect – 'games' and 'puzzles' are dreadfully low-brow terms – but my hope here, as in the rest of the book, is simply to demonstrate the delicious variety of pleasures that can be enjoyed by those who travel through the world of English words.

Word Entertainments

Acrostics

An acrostic is a verse in which the initial letters of the lines form words. Lewis Carroll loved creating acrostics and here is his most famous example, dedicated to Alice Pleasaunce Liddell, the little girl who inspired *Alice's Adventures in Wonderland*:

A boat, beneath a sunny sky
Lingering onward dreamily
In an evening of July –

Children three that nestle near,
Eager eye and willing ear,
Pleased a simple tale to hear –

Long has paled that sunny sky:
Echoes fade and memories die:
Autumn frosts have slain July.

Still she haunts me, phantomwise,
Alice moving under skies
Never seen by waking eyes.

Children yet the tale to hear,
Eager eye and willing ear,
Lovingly shall nestle near.

In Wonderland they lie,
Dreaming as the days go by,
Dreaming as the summers die:

Ever drifting down the stream –
Lingering in the golden gleam –
Life, what is it but a dream?

A double acrostic is one in which the initial and the final
letters of the lines make up words, and a triple acrostic is one
in which the initial letters, the final letters and a middle letter
of each line make up words. A telestich is an even more
complex relation of the acrostic, in which the initial letters of
the lines spell one word, while the final letters of the lines spell
another word with a meaning contrary to the first! Here is a
neat Victorian example, using the words 'unite' and 'untie'
and so adding a pleasing anagrammatical dimension to the
whole!

Unite and untie are the same – so say yoU,
Not in wedlock, I ween, has this unity beeN.
In the drama of marriage each wandering gouT
To a new face would fly – all except you and I –
Each seeking to alter the spell in their scenE.

Alphabetics

In 1842 *The Times* carried this unusual advertisement:

To widowers and single gentlemen – wanted
by a lady, a *Situation* to superintend the
household and preside at table. She is
Agreeable, Becoming, Careful, Desirable,
English, Facetious, Generous, Honest, Industrious,
Keen, Lively, Merry, Natty, Obedient,
Philosophic, Quiet, Regular, Sociable,
Tasteful, Useful, Vivacious, Womanish,
Xantippish, Youthful, Zealous, etc.

The lady in question was obviously a prize worth winning, for as well as all her stated virtues she was also a mistress of the art of Alphabetics. To master the art yourself all you need to do is devise an essay or a poem or a story or an advertisement in which each word begins with a successive letter of the alphabet. It can even be done with a toast, as the Jacobite, Lord Duff, showed in 1745 when he called on those around him to raise their glasses to this alphabet:

ABC	A Blessed Change
DEF	Down Every Foreigner
GHJ	God Help James
KLM	Keep Lord Marr
NOP	Noble Ormond Preserve
QRS	Quickly Resolve Stewart
TUVW	Truss Up Vile Whigs
XYZ	'Xert Your Zeal!

The toast, of course, contains a hidden 'I' in that it has been merged with 'J'. This was an excusable practice in 1745, but in a modern Alphabetic exercise all 26 letters must be included.

Anagrams

When you have turned the word 'scythe' into the word 'chesty' simply by rearranging the letters, you have created an anagram. It isn't a very interesting anagram because 'scythe' and 'chesty' don't have anything in common. For an anagram to be fun, the rearranged letters should relate in some way to the original word. Here are some fine examples from the unique anagram library of the American authority, Mr Dmitri Borgmann:

CONVERSATION	VOICES RANT ON
DESPERATION	A ROPE ENDS IT
PUNISHMENT	NINE THUMPS
ENDEARMENTS	TENDER NAMES
STEAMER	SEA TERM
WAITRESS	A STEW, SIR?
FAMILIES	LIFE'S AIM
PROSECUTORS	COURT POSERS
TWINGES	WESTING

From the same splendid collection come these anagrams which are based on phrases rather than single words:

A DECIMAL POINT	A DOT IN PLACE
THE COUNTRYSIDE	NO CITY DUST HERE
THE NUDIST COLONY	NO UNTIDY CLOTHES
A SENTENCE OF DEATH	FACES ONE AT THE END
THE UNITED STATES OF AMERICA	ATTAINETH ITS CAUSE: FREEDOM
THE LEANING TOWER OF PISA	WHAT A FOREIGN STONE PILE
A SHOPLIFTER	HAS TO PILFER
ONE HUG	ENOUGH?
THE EYES	THEY SEE
THE MONA LISA	NO HAT, A SMILE

The names of the great and famous can sometimes make telling anagrams. Here are two based on the name 'William Shakespeare':

I ASK ME, HAS WILL A PEER?
WE ALL MAKE HIS PRAISE

Bomb Shelter...

And here are three devised by Lewis Carroll. The first two come from the name of one of Carroll's least favourite statesman, William Ewart Gladstone, and the third is based on the name 'Florence Nightingale':

WILD AGITATOR! MEANS WELL
WILT TEAR DOWN *ALL* IMAGES?
FLIT ON, CHEERING ANGEL!

For a versified use of anagrams, it would be hard to improve on this version of an old bit of British doggerel, by American writer Martin Gardner; here only the letters, E, I, L, and V are used to form six different words:

A VILE young lady on EVIL bent,
Lowered her VEIL with sly intent.
'LEVI,' she said, 'It's time to play.
What shall we do to LIVE today?
'My dear,' said he, 'do as you please.
'*I'm* going to eat some IVEL cheese!'

Antigrams

No, antigrams aren't cables you send to maiden aunts: they are anagrams with a difference. In an antigram, the word of words created out of the letters in the original word have a meaning opposite to the meaning of the original word. For example, 'evil's agents' is a neat antigram for 'evangelists'. Here are some other examples of word antigrams taken from Mr Dmitri Borgmann's collection:

MISFORTUNE	IT'S MORE FUN
FUNERAL	REAL FUN
SANTA	SATAN
ENORMITY	MORE TINY
INFECTION	FINE TONIC
MILITARISM	I LIMIT ARMS
FILLED	ILL-FED
VIOLENCE	NICE LOVE
RESTFUL	FLUSTER
MARITAL	MARTIAL

And from the same source, here are four antigrams based on phrases rather than single words:

A TRAGEDY	RATED GAY
A PICTURE OF HEALTH	OFT PALE, I ACHE, HURT
OLD MAN WINTER	WARM, INDOLENT
THE MAN WHO LAUGHS	HE'S GLUM, WON'T HA-HA

Logograms

Officially, a logogram is 'a sign representing a word in short-hand'. Unofficially, logograms are word puzzles in which a word changes its meaning as it loses certain of its letters. Here is a straight-forward example:

Beginning with a fruit you move to the part of a kitchen where you cook and go on to do what the telephone did and then what the four-minute miler did before becoming a Sun god and an indefinite article.

The word you are looking for is ORANGE, which becomes other words as you drop each letter in turn:

ORANGE
RANGE
RANG
RA
A

Here is a versified logogram from the pen of Lord Macaulay:

> Cut off my head, how singular I act!
>   Cut off my tail, and plural I appear,
> Cut off my head and tail – most curious fact! –
>   Although my middle's left, there's nothing there!
> What is my head cut off? A sounding sea!
>   What is my tail cut off? A flowing river!
> Amid their mingling depths I fearless play,
>   Parent of softest sounds, though mute for ever!

The starting word in Macaulay's logogram is, as you will have worked out by now, COD.

Malapropisms

If there were any justice in the world of words, malapropisms would have been named after Shakespeare's Constable Dogberry rather than Sheridan's Mrs Malaprop. Here is Dogberry instructing his watchmen in *Much Ado About Nothing*:

DOGBERRY You are thought here to be the most senseless and fit man for the constable of the watch, therefore bear you the lantern. This is your charge: you shall comprehend all vagrom men: you are to bid any man stand, in the prince's name.

WATCH How, if a'well not stand?

DOGBERRY Why, then, take no note of him, but let him go; and presently call the rest of the watch together and thank God you are rid of a knave . . . You shall also make no noise in the streets; for, for the watch to babble and to talk is most tolerable and not to be endured.

And here are a few edited highlights from the small-talk of Mrs Malaprop herself in *The Rivals*:

As headstrong as an allegory on the banks of the Nile.
Illiterate him, I say, quite from your memory.
If I reprehend anything in this world, it is the use of
my oracular tongue, and a nice derangement of
epitaphs.

Much more recently, Norton Mockridge noted some
even more ludicrous misuses of language in his *Fractured
English*. Here is a small sampling:

I was so surprised you could have knocked me over
    with a fender.
It sure is good to be back on terracotta again.
A wealthy typhoon.
My sister uses massacre on her eyes.
White as the dripping snow.
Everything is going to rot and ruin.
He used biceps to deliver the baby.
My father is retarded on a pension.
Frances has beautiful hands, and some day I'm going
    to make a bust of them.
The English language is going through a resolution.

Metagrams

A metagram is a word which can be turned into a number of
other words by the simple process of changing its initial letter.
KINK is a perfect metagram as you can see:

KINK
LINK
MINK
PINK
RINK
SINK
WINK

CAN is another, with even greater potential, as this late-Victorian verse reveals:

A vessel, when empty I make a great sound	CAN!
For frying I'm used, in shape I am round	PAN!
My lady she carries me off in her hand	FAN!
All the boys did it when they heard the band	RAN!
The king of creation, and proud of his race	MAN!
A pretty girl's name if it's short's no disgrace	NAN!
The law on the rebel laid me, alack	BAN!
I'm an old Jewish tribe that existed long back	DAN!
The sun takes your faces and paints them with me	TAN!
Where the brave soldier stands, who never would flee	VAN!

Mixed Metaphors

A mixed metaphor is a figure of speech that combines two or more inconsistent metaphors. The classic example comes in the fourth line of Hamlet's famous soliloquy: 'Or to take arms against a sea of troubles.'

Lesser fry than Shakespeare have come up with even more mixed metaphors. Here is Ian Fleming: 'Bond's knees, the Achilles heel of all skiers, were beginning to ache.' Here is Ernest Bevin: 'If you let that sort of thing go on, your bread and butter will be cut from under your feet.' And here is an Irish politician, Sir Boyle Roche: 'Mr Speaker, I smell a rat; I see him forming in the air and darkening the sky; but I'll nip him in the bud!'

Other famous, if non-attributable, mixed metaphors include: 'The skeleton at the feast was a mare's nest.' 'We're not out of the wood yet by a long chalk.' 'All these whited sepulchres are tarred with the same brush.' As you can tell, they're all pearls worth their weight in gold.

Mnemonics

The mnemonic, named after Mnemosyne, the goddess of

memory, is a system to help you remember things and there are more or less effective examples in every kind of discipline.

Here is a mnemonic that will help you remember the names of a frog's arteries, in the order in which they branch off the main aorta:

*L*ittle *m*en *i*n *s*hort *b*lack *m*ackintoshes

Lingula, mandibular, innominate, subclavian, brachial and musculo-cutaneous are the arteries the mnemonic helps brings to mind.

Here is one that will help you get the order of battles of the Wars of the Roses:

A boy *n*ow *w*ill *m*ention *a*ll *t*he *h*ot, *h*orrid *b*attles *t*ill Bosworth

And this is the order of the battles in longhand: St *A*lbans, *B*lore Heath, *N*orthampton, *W*akefield, *M*ortimer's Cross, the Second Battle of St *A*lbans, *T*owton, *H*edgeley Moor, *H*exham, *B*arnet, *T*ewkesbury, *B*osworth.

To bring the vertebral bones of the spinal column to mind (the cervical, dorsal, lumbar, sacrum and coccyx), this is your mnemonic:

*C*lever *D*ick *l*ooks *s*illy *c*lot

For the geological periods in descending order of age (Cambrian, Ordovician, Silurian, Devonian, Carboniferous, Permian, Triassic, Jurassic, Cretaceous, Eocene, Oligocene, Miocene, Pliocene, Pleistocene, Recent), try this mnemonic:

*C*amels *o*ften *s*it *d*own *c*arefully. *P*erhaps *t*heir *j*oints *c*reak? *E*arly *o*iling *m*ight *p*revent *p*ermanent *r*heumatism

This is known as the nanny's mnemonic:

*H*ideous *f*ools, *m*orons, *k*eep *s*ilent!

Far from the phrase representing nanny's attitude towards her employers, it reminds her of the items she should check when making sure her charges are presentable:

*H*air brushed?
*F*ace washed?
*M*iddle neat?
*K*nees clean?
*S*hoes brushed and tied?

This is the drinking man's mnemonic:

Beer on whisky very risky.
Whisky on beer never fear.

As poetry it may not amount to much, but it should help you avoid a hangover.

Monosyllabics

Many of the words we use contain just one syllable. Many more contain more. When we write and speak we almost always use both monosyllabic words, but the wordsmith who is fascinated by monosyllabics does his best to use only words of one syllable when he writes and speaks. It isn't easy. As an exercise, try to write a sensible sentence consisting entirely of monosyllabics. If you do it with ease, try writing a poem in the same way. Here is a monosyllabic verse from the seventeenth-century lyric poet, Robert Herrick, to show you how it can be done:

THE DAFFODILS

We have short time to stay as you,
We have as short a spring;
As quick a growth to meet decay
As you or anything.
We die
As your hours do, and dry
Like the rain,
Or as the pearls of dew.

Herrick slips up once by using the word 'decay' in the third line. Gyles Brandreth, in this pithy poem, doesn't slip up at all. It is a perfect example of monosyllabic verse:

ODE TO MY LATE LAMENTED GOLDFISH
O
Wet
Pet!

Multitudes

As everyone knows, a flock of ships is called a fleet and a fleet of sheep is called a flock. Not everyone is familiar with all the other collective nouns. With how many of these are you familiar:

A colony of ants
A shrewdness of apes
A cete of badgers
A shoal of bass
A sloth of bears
An army of caterpillars
A clowder of cats
A drove of cattle
A peep of chickens
A murder of crows
A dule of doves
A balding of ducks*
A clutch of eggs
A school of fish
A skulk of foxes
A gaggle of geese†
A husk of hares
A cast of hawks
A brood of hens
A siege of herons

A harras of horses
A smack of jellyfish
A kindle of kittens
A deceit of lapwings
An exaltation of larks
A leap of leopards
A pride of lions
A plague of locusts
A watch of nightingales
A parliament of owls
A covey of partridges
An ostentation of peacocks
A congregation of plovers
A string of ponies
A litter of puppies
A nest of rabbits
An unkindness of ravens
A crash of rhinoceroses
A building of rooks
A pod of seals

*It's a paddling of ducks when the ducks are on the water.
†It's a skein of geese when the geese are in flight.

A flock of sheep	A hover of trout
A host of sparrows	A rafter of turkeys
A dray of squirrels	A pitying of turtledoves
A murmuration of starlings	A bale of turtles
A mustering of storks	A gam of whales
A flight of swallows	A route of wolves
A knot of toads	A descent of woodpeckers

Those are some 'official' collective nouns. If you feel you can improve on them (a picnic of bears, a cluck of chickens, a coat of doves, a gulp of swallows, a jonah of whales, a tin of sardines) have a go.

Palindromes

If it's true that they spoke English in the Garden of Eden, then it's certain that 'Madam, I'm Adam' was the first palindrome. If they didn't, then it is possible that the Greek poet, Sotades, is the man responsible for devising the original palindrome.

A palindrome is a word (such as 'deed or 'level' or 'repayer' or 'noon' or 'nun') or a phrase or a sentence (such as 'Madam, I'm Adam') that reads the same backwards as forwards. John Taylor is credited with having created the first English palindrome at the beginning of the seventeenth century:

Lewd did I live & evil I did dwel.

It was considered a perfect palindrome at the time, but spelling habits have changed since, so that a more acceptable version of the same palindrome today would read:

Evil I did dwell; lewd did I live.

Here are some other, more recent, palindromes:

Was it a car or a cat I saw?
Pull up if I pull up.

Ten animals I slam in a net.
In a regal age ran I.
Yawn a more Roman way.
Some men interpret nine memos.

A lot of palindromes involve people's names, some of them quite famous ones:

Was it Eliot's toilet I saw?
No mists reign at Tangier, St Simon!
Sums are not set as a test on Erasmus.

And some are supposed to have been spoken by the famous. The composer, Henry Purcell, is said to have remarked:

Egad, a base tone denotes a bad age!

And it is well known that the Emperor Napoleon was wont to moan during his exile:

Able was I ere I saw Elba.

For a modern palindrome that succinctly tells a story, it would be hard to beat this one by Leigh Mercer, a master palindromist:

A man, a plan, a canal – Panama.

The American wit and versifier, Willard Espy, reported an entertaining interview in the *Harvard Bulletin* between 'Professor R Oseforp, holder of the Emor D Nilap Chair in Palindromology at Harvard, and Solomon W Golomb PhD '57' in which the reply to every question was a neat palindrome:

'And what about your new novel, could you tell me the
title?'
'Dennis Sinned.'
'Intriguing. What is the plot?'
'Dennis and Edna sinned.'
'I see. Is there more to it than that?'
'Dennis Krats and Edna Stark sinned.'
'Now it all becomes clear,' I agreed. 'Tell me, with all this
concern about the economy, what kind of car are you
driving nowadays?'
'A Toyota.'
'Naturally, and how about your colleague, Professor
Nustad?'
'Nustad? A Datsun.'

Not as difficult to devise, but just as entertaining to read
are palindromes where the words as entities, and not individual letters, can be read forwards or backwards in the same
sentence. Here are four prize-winning entries from a *New
Statesman* competition:

Women understand men; few men understand women.
God knows man. What is doubtful is what man knows
     God.
Does milk machinery milk does?
Bores are people that say that people are bores.

Pangrams

When reading the Book of Ezra, Chapter 7, Verse 21, you
will have been struck by this sentence: 'And I, even I Artax-
erxes the king, do make a decree to all the treasurers which
are beyond the river, that whatsoever Ezra the priest, the
scribe of the laws of the God of heaven, shall require of you, it
be done speedily.' The sentence is *almost* a pangram. Had it

included the letter 'j' it would have been one, because a
pangram is a sentence that includes every letter of the
alphabet.

Here is a rather shorter pangram, consisting of just 48
letters:

> John P Brady gave me a black walnut box of quite a
> small size.

Here is another even shorter one. It consists of only 33
letters and is often used by trainee typists who are trying to get
to know all the letters on the keyboard:

> A quick brown fox jumps over the lazy dog.

This pangram is even more concise, consisting of 32
letters:

Pack my box with five dozen liquor jugs.

Once you get down to 29 and 28 letters you have got to
bring in names to help you out:

> Quick wafting zephyrs vex bold Jim.
> Waltz, nymph, for quick jigs vex Bud.

The only way to create a 26-letter pangram is to invent
funny names to use up some of the letters, like this:

> J Q Schwartz flung D V Pike my box.

If you think you can devise a 26-letter pangram that
doesn't use proper names of any kind, let us know. You will
be the first person ever to have done so.

Paragrams

Homonyms are words that are spelt alike but mean different things. For example, because trees have barks and so do dogs, because rivers have banks and so do people with money, because girls can be fair and children love fun fairs, 'bark' and 'bank' and 'fair' are homonyms. Homophones are words that sound alike but are spelt differently and mean different things. Bare and bear, boy and buoy, cereal and serial, knead and need, him and hymn, right and rite and write, are all homophones.

Homonyms and homophones play an important part in punning and in the creation of ingenious word puzzles called paragrams, in which one word plays many parts. Towards which words does this paragrammatic verse lead you:

> To season Folly's synonym I'm used,
> Although I'm wise as everyone can tell,
> The seasoned one, perchance, has been abused,
> For once in Rome she proved her wisdom well.

The homonyms in question here are the words *sage* and *goose*, the sage being both the seasoning for goose and the name given to a wise person, and the goose being both the name given to someone who is a bit of a fool and the feathered bird whose cackling, historians will recall, once roused the sentinel in Rome and so saved the Capitol.

Puns

The glorious paradox of the pun is that the worse it is the better it is. When you have heard a pleasing pun you don't show your appreciation by laughing; you groan instead. Puns are plays on words using the same or similar sounds and they come in all shapes and sizes. There are heavenly puns:

> Saint Peter: And how did you get here?
> Latest arrival: 'Flu!'

And hellish puns:

> Latest arrival: Do you mind if I smoke?
> Little devil: I don't mind if you burn!

There are clever puns:

> Ladies and gentlemen, I give you a toast.
> It is, 'Absinthe makes the tart grow fonder!'

And not-so-clever puns:

> 'Waiter, this coffee tastes like mud!'
> 'I'm sorry sir. It was only ground this morning.'

There are philosophic puns:

> Better to have loved a short girl,
> Than never to have loved a tall.

And versified puns:

> When I am dead I hope it may be said:
> 'His sins were scarlet, but his books were read.'
> *Hilaire Belloc*

Since 'Peter' meant 'rock' in Greek, Jesus obviously knew how to pun when he declared that 'upon this rock' he intended to build his church. Few great writers have resisted altogether the temptation to indulge in the occasional pun and some, like Shakespeare, revelled in it. 'Ask for me tomorrow and you shall find me a grave man,' says Mercutio as he is about to die.

One- and two-word puns, like the Scotsman's definition of porridge ('oat cuisins'), are common. Harder to come by are puns that parallel a complete phrase. They usually require a reasonably complex build-up. For example, with the words and music of 'We're rolling along on the crest of a wave!' firmly in mind, picture two Roman warriors standing over a prostrate slave and holding an enormous gong on the slave's naked torso. As you will have guessed by now, they're singing: 'We're rolling a gong on the chest of a slave!'

The American humorist, Bennett Cerf, did even better when he recounted the tale of the detective hired to unearth a certain missing person, a Mr Rhee by name, who happened to work for *Life* magazine in New York. When the detective eventually came across the man, he was happy to exclaim: 'Ah, sweet Mr Rhee of *Life*, at last I've found you!'

The longer the pun the more contrived it is likely to be and spontaneous puns are usually the most satisfying. For example, this exchange between Mr Justice Darling and F E Smith actually took place in court and is a fine example of 'punning on one's feet':

Mr Justice Darling: And who is George Robey?
F E Smith: He is the Darling of the music halls, m'lud.

If punning is not a sport to your liking, don't worry. It's well known that one man's Mede is another man's Persian.

Riddles

Using homonyms, homophones and puns, riddles are puzzles that can fascinate and infuriate. Here are a few old favourites to give a flavour of the genre:

Hairy Chest..

Q. What grammatical term is least liked by young lovers?
A. The third person.

Q. In what sort of syllables ought a parrot to speak?
A. In polly-syllables.

Q. When can you recognize the naked truth?
A. When you are given the bare facts.

Q. In what colour should a secret be kept?
A. Inviolate.

Q. When is longhand quicker than shorthand?
A. When it is on a clock.

Q. Why is a crossword puzzle like a quarrel?
A. Because one word leads to another.

Q. Why is a joke like a coconut?
A. Because it is of no use until it has been cracked.

Q. Why does a dishonest man stay indoors?
A. So that no one will find him out.

Q. When is a farmer best able to look at his pigs?
A. When he has a sty in his eye.

Q. Why are playing cards like wolves?
A. Because they come in packs.

Semordnilaps

Most people wouldn't know a semordnilap if they fell over one. Here is a good selection for you to fall over:

BARD
DESSERT
DEVIL
DOG
MAPS
MOOD
REKNITS
REDRAWER
REPAID
STRAW
STRAP
STOP

If you haven't yet spotted what the dozen words have in common, take a closer look at the word 'semordnilap'. Yes, you've got it! It's 'palindromes' spelt backwards and, in the same way that a palindromic word reads the same backwards as forwards, a semordnilapic word becomes a new word when spelt backwards. As we have seen, palindromic sentences are famous, but curiously, semordnilapic sentences are almost unheard of. As a cure for insomnia, you might try to devise one.

Spoonerisms

The chances are you will never have heard of metaphasis. The chances are you will have heard of spoonerisms. Both amount to the same thing: an accidental transposition of the initial letters of the words in a phrase so as to change the phrase's meaning or make a nonsense of it. Here are some choice examples.

You have tasted a whole worm.
You have hissed my mystery lectures.
You were fighting a liar in the quadrangle.
You will leave by the town drain.
I have just received a blushing crow.
Let us toast the queer old dean!

These classic spoonerisms have all been attributed to Dr William Spooner, Warden of New College, Oxford, 1903–1924. He is supposed to have got up in Chapel one day and announced the next hymn as 'Kinquering Kongs their titles take' and in doing so to have created the original spoonerism. Alas, he did no such thing. Nor did he utter any of the other gems, traditionally attributed to him. However, on concluding a sermon he did once say, 'In the sermon I have just preached, whenever I said Aristotle I meant St Paul,' and he did once admit to looking 'in a dark, glassly', and, whether deservedly or not, he has become known as the creator of the spoonerism, so we are justified in calling these further examples of metaphasis spine foonerisms:

> For real enjoyment, give me a well-boiled icycle.
> Is it kisstomary to cuss the bride?
> It's roaring with pain outside.
> May I sew you to another sheet?

Word Games

Alphabet Race

This is a paper and pencil game for two players in which they race to see who can use all 26 letters of the alphabet first. Each player has a piece of paper on which he has written out the complete alphabet and there is a third piece of paper which serves as the 'board'. The players take it in turn to write words on the board, making sure that the word they play attaches at some point to a word already played. A player can only use each letter once and when he has written it on the board he must cross it off his list. For example, if the opening player begins by writing OPEN on the board, he then crosses the letters O, P, E, and N off his list. His opponent must now write a word that he can attach to OPEN, for example ZOO:

z
o
OPEN

He now crosses the letters z and o off his list because they are the two letters he has played.

The player to use all 26 of his letters first wins the game. If a stage is reached when neither player can play, the player who has used most of his letters at that point is the winner. The words themselves don't score points: the sole aim of the game is to be the first one to use up the alphabet.

Here is how the board might look at the end of a game. The first player's words are written in capitals. His opponent's words are in lower case letters.

```
      d            W
    fur           IF
    m        cable
    p         h    L   Z
    SCYTHE        Dozing
             s        X  P
             t
          YOUNG
             R
          WAX
             B
```

When the stalemate was reached, the player using capitals still had five letters unused and the player using lower case letters had only four, thus becoming the winner.

Animal Magic

Equip all the players with pencil and paper and give them ten minutes in which to write down all the adjectives they can think of that have their origin in birds and beasts but which, as adjectives, can be applied to human beings. Here are some examples:

Asinine	Fishy
Batty	Foxy
Bitchy	Lousy
Bovine	Mulish
Catty	Ratty
Cocky	Sheepish
Crabby	Sluggish
Dogged	Swinish
Elephantine	Waspish

When the time is up the player with the longest list of adjectives wins the game.

Since, curiously, so many of the adjectives refer to what are generally regarded as unpleasant or unattractive characteristics, any player who manages to include adjectives that have a pleasant connotation ('kittenish' for example) will be allowed to count that one adjective as two.

Backwards Spelling

At the best of times, spelling words like *Parallel, Separate, Embarrassed, Ellipse, Erratically, Correspondence* and *Battalion* presents all but a few of us with problems. Spelling the words *backwards* would seem to be asking altogether too much – but that's just what this amusing parlour game is all about.

The players take it in turn to be given a word and have to spell it backwards. They must start to speak as soon as they have been told the word and they must not hesitate or correct themselves while they are speaking. Every time a player spells a word backwards correctly he scores a point. After ten rounds, the player with the highest score is the winner.

Inexperienced players will find even the simplest six- and seven-letter words a challenge and everyone will find words like these nearly impossible:

Abbreviation	Noncomformity
Blunderbuss	Onomatopoeia
Dilatory	Quintessential
Evangelistic	Rumbustious
Fluorescence	Scatological
Graphology	Tautological
Helter Skelter	Unintentional
Ingratiating	Vaporousness
Juvenescence	Whomsoever
Kaleidoscope	Yarborough
Laryngitis	Zincograph

An umpire should be appointed before the game begins to select the words to be spelt and to make sure that they are being spelt backwards in the correct order.

Build-up

The players are given a simple word onto which they must build up as many other words as they can think of. For example, if the given word is HEAD here are just some of the words that can be built up from it: headhunter, headmaster, head-over-heels, headstrong, headlong, headmistress, head-quarters, headdress, headline, heading, heady, headache, headfast, header, headmost, headsman, headband, head-gear.

If the players are given a set time limit, say five or ten minutes, the player with the longest list when the time is up is the winner of the game.

To give the players even greater scope, as well as starting with short words that can be built up into longer ones, it is possible to start with prefixes. Here, for example, is a *very* small selection of the words you can build up from EX: exacerbate, exact, exactly, exaggerate, exalt, examination, example, exasperate, excavate, exceed, excel, except, exhibit, exhilarate, exhortation, exigence, exiguous, exile, exist, exit, exorbitant, exotic, expand, expatiate.

Five by Five

This is a paper and pencil game for two players. Each player draws a grid five letters wide, five deep on a piece of paper.

The players do not let each other see their own grids until the game is over.

The two players take it in turn to call out letters. When a player calls out a letter he puts it into one of the squares on his grid. His opponent must also put the called-out letter somewhere on his grid. This continues until the first player has called out thirteen letters and his opponent has called out twelve, when the two grids will be full.

The object of the exercise is to fill your own grid with three-, four-, and five-letter words going horizontally and vertically. At the end of the game you will score three points for every three-letter word, four for every four-letter word and five for every five-letter word, so the letters you call out will be ones designed to help you make words in your grid. Your opponent, of course, will have to accommodate the letters you call out in his grid as best he can. When he calls out his letters they will be the ones he thinks will help him make words for his grid and you will then have to try to make the most of the letters he gives you.

Here is what the two grids looked like at the end of a game between Adam and Eve, in which Adam called out the letters R, G, E, L, A, S, O, L, I, P, E, L and S, and Eve called out A, N, C, H, O, R, E, A, E, N, D and V.

Adam's grid					Eve's grid			
R	A	N	C	H	G	R	A	P	E
O	G	R	E	A	R	O	E	L	A
P	E	E	L	S	O	L	V	I	C
E	N	D	L	V	A	L	E	E	H
S	O	L	I	A	N	S	N	D	S

Here is what each player scored:

ADAM: *Words across* RANCH(5), OGRE(4), PEELS(5), END(3): *Words down* ROPES(5) AGE(3), RED(3), CELL(4), HAS(3). Total 35 points.

EVE: *Words across* GRAPE(5), ROE(3), ALE(3); *Words down* GROAN(5), ROLLS(5), EVEN(4), PLIED(5), EACH(4). Total 34 points. Adam has won the game by just one point, so he is allowed to start the next game.

One- and two-letter words don't count and each letter can only be counted once in either direction. For example, in her top horizontal line, Eve can only score for GRAPE, she cannot also score for RAPE, RAP or APE.

To add an extra dimension to the game, a bonus of ten points can be awarded to any player who manages to form a five-letter word running diagonally from the top left-hand corner of his grid to the bottom right-hand corner.

Fore and Aft

In this game you and the other players are given five minutes in which to write down a list of words that begin and end with the same letter. Here are some examples: area, aria; clinic, cardiac; evasive, escape; gag, groaning; kirk, kink; mum, minimum; plump, pop; stress, sometimes; yearly.

Naturally, you increase the potential number of words if you allow proper names (Cadillac, Xerox), foreign words (Uhuru), colloquialisms (zizz) and exclamations (Aha! Wow!) and you make the game a lot easier (and much more time-consuming) if you allow the players to consult dictionaries.

When the players have all had the set time for writing out their lists, the player with the longest list of acceptable words beginning and ending with the same letter is the winner. You can also play the game as a form of solitaire and simply do your best to think of the longest list of words possible.

Four-letter Word Game

In the now accepted sense of the word, this is a *nice* game despite its name. Any number can play and all each player needs is paper, pencil and a vocabulary of one-, two-, three- and four-letter words.

The players are given a set period of time, say fifteen minutes, in which to write a simple story using only words with four or fewer letters. At the end of the time limit, the players read out their stories and the player who has written the longest, most lucid and entertaining story is the winner.

It sounds simple, but it isn't—especially when you remember that one five-letter word inadvertently slipped in will mean that you are disqualified. Here is a brief Love Story to give you an idea of the game's scope – and its limitations:

Love Story

It was in May a year or two ago that I met the fair Miss Anne Bun. She was just a slip of a girl and I was a man on the edge of ripe old age. We had tea on that cool May morn on the lawn at her Pa's seat near Deal by the sea. She was gay and full of life. I was grey and full of woe, but she did not seem to mind. I do not feel she fell in love with me just so that she and her vile Mama were to be able to have the vast sums of cash that I keep in a bank in town. She said that from the time she was a baby her wish had been to meet a man with a leg made of wood and a red wig and that she was full of joy that at long last I had come to her. Yes, she said, to be my one and only wife was what she did want – and so did her Mama. (Her Papa was deaf and so had no say in the case, poor soul.) If I gave her all my cash she would give me all her love. It was a fair deal and I was keen to say yes, but fate took a hand and said no, Miss Anne Bun is not to be your wife. She is to be run over by a big red bus on her way to the wee kirk on the hill. And that is what came to pass, alas, so that is the end of my sad tale. Take pity on me and weep for me as I lie all on my own in my old man's bed with only the idea of my lost love by me.

Ghost

There are few games that can sort out those with impressive vocabularies from those without as well as the game of Ghost. It is a word game for two or more players in which the players build up a series of letters to form a word but endeavour not to be the player that finishes a word.

The first player begins by calling out a letter. The second player adds a second letter to the first, making sure that the two-letter combination could actually begin a real word. The third player adds a third letter, again thinking of a real word.

The fourth player adds a fourth, and so it goes on around the group until one of the players is forced to finish a word in which case that player has lost the game.

Players must at all times have a real word in mind and a player can challenge the player he follows if he feels that that player did not have a word in mind when he added his letter. If the challenger is correct and the player did not have a proper word in mind, the player that added the wrong letter loses the game. If he did have a proper word in mind, it is the challenger who loses the game. Three-letter words don't count.

Here is an example, as played by Tom, Dick and Harry:

TOM A (He is thinking of APPLE)

DICK AR (He is thinking of AREA)

HARRY ARC (Although ARC is a word it does not eliminate Harry because three-letter words don't count and he is thinking of ARCH)

TOM ARCA (He is thinking of ARCADE)

DICK ARCAN (He is thinking of ARCANUM)

HARRY (He cannot think of a letter to follow ARCAN and so challenges Dick because he is sure Dick only said N because he couldn't think of anything better to say! However Dick, when challenged, reveals that ARCA-NUM was the word he had in mind and the dictionary confirms that an ARCANUM is a 'mystery' or 'secret', a perfectly legitimate word for Dick to use, so Harry loses the game.)

Here is a two-handed game played between Adam and Eve:

ADAM G (He is thinking of GOAT)

EVE GL (She is thinking of GLASS)

ADAM GLO (He is thinking of GLOAT)

EVE GLOB (She is thinking of GLOBE)

ADAM GLOBU (He is thinking of GLOBULE)

EVE GLOBUL (She is thinking of GLOBULIN)

ADAM GLOBULA (He is thinking of GLOBULAR)

EVE GLOBULAR (She added the final R to GLOBULAR and lost the game because she knew she had no alternative.)

Superghost

Superghost is Ghost for masterminds. The principle of the game is the same. The difference is that in Superghost players can add their letters to either end of the group of letters as it is being built up! It is only to be played when you have mastered all the intricacies of Ghost and learnt the *Shorter Oxford English Dictionary* off by heart, as you can see from this game played by Adam and Eve.

ADAM R (He is thinking of RICE)

EVE RO (She is thinking of ROSE)

adam TRO (He is thinking of TROUBLE)

EVE NTRO (She is thinking of UNTROUBLED)

ADAM ONTRO (He is thinking of CONTROVERSY)

EVE CONTRO (She is thinking of CONTROL)

ADAM NCONTRO (He is thinking of UNCONTROLLED)

EVE NCONTROV (She is thinking of UNCONTRO-VERSIAL)

ADAM NCONTROVE (He is thinking of UNCONTRO-VERSIAL too)

EVE NCONTROVER (She is thinking of UNCONTRO-VERSIAL still)

ADAM INCONTROVER (He has just realized that if they continue with UNCONTROVERSIAL he will lose the game, so he is now thinking of INCONTRO-VERTIBLE)

EVE INCONTROVERT (She has realized that she too must change to INCONTROVERTIBLE and that the result of the game is now a foregone conclusion.)

ADAM INCONTROVERTI

EVE INCONTROVERTIB

ADAM INCONTROVERTIBL
EVE INCONTROVERTIBLE

I Love My Love

In the traditional version of this game the players take it in turn to describe their loved one using different letters of the alphabet, like this:

TOM I love my love with an A because she is April from Adelaide and altogether adorable.

DICK I love my love with a B because she is Brenda from Birmingham and breathtakingly beautiful.

HARRY I love my love with a C because she is Charlotte from Cardiff and completely charming.

In the wordsmith's version of the game the players continue with the same letter of the alphabet until they have exhausted it. Starting at A they take it in turn to think of adjectives beginning with A to describe their loved one and go on and on until one of them cannot think of a fresh adjective beginning with A or inadvertently repeats himself. He loses a point and all the players move on to the next letter. When the players have reached the letter Z or have decided to stop play after eight hours having only reached C, the player who has lost least points becomes the winner.

For those with rich vocabularies (and for those seeking to acquire them) this is a very entertaining game, as you can see from the first moments of this contest between Tom, Dick and Harry:

TOM I love my love with an A because she is Abandoned!
DICK Able!
HARRY Amiable!
TOM Artful!
DICK Accommodating!

HARRY Acceptable!
TOM Accomplished!
DICK Adulterous!
HARRY Advanced!
TOM Affluent!
DICK Affable!
HARRY Amorous!
TOM Aristocratic!
DICK Average!
HARRY Available!
TOM Autonomous!
DICK Autocratic!
HARRY Authoritative!
TOM Authentic!
DICK Awe-inspiring!
HARRY Awake!
TOM Astonishing!
DICK Angelic!
HARRY Altruistic!
TOM Almond-eyed!
DICK Arduous!
HARRY Aromatic!
TOM Abandoned!

By making his love 'abandoned' Tom has repeated one of the attributes already ascribed to her, so the time has come to move on to B and we shall never know whether the young lady was also antiseptic, assuaging, anti-Semitic and amphibious or not.

The Initial Letter Game

'Delightful, delicious, delectable, dainty Deborah Diamanté, dare-devil Danny Diamanté's dimpled daughter, demanded desperate decisions . . .' That is the intriguing opening of one player's effort in the Initial Letter Game, the aim of which is to write the longest story using words beginning with only one letter.

You can play the game on your own as a form of mental gymnastics, or you can equip all the players with pencil and paper and give them ten minutes in which to concoct their stories. When the time is up, the player with the longest story that makes sense and only features words beginning with the given letter wins the game.

A, B, C, D, E, F, G, H, L, M, N, R, S, T and W are the letters to use. If you try playing with the others, the game is almost impossible.

One Hundred Words

Could you write a hundred words that made sense and not repeat a single word once? If you can, then you have mastered the game already because that's all it involves. Here is how Mrs Pearl Feldman and her pupils managed at Pompton Lakes High School, New Jersey, USA, where the game originated:

Let's go! The challenge is to write a composition without using any word more than once. Do you think that it can be done? If not, give one reason for doing this. While we are sitting here in English class at Pompton Lakes High School, Lakeside Avenue, New Jersey, all of us figure out something which makes sense. Mrs Feldman helps her pupils because another teacher said they couldn't accomplish such tasks. Nobody has fresh ideas right now. Goal – 100! How far did students get? Eighty-five done already; fifteen left. 'Pretty soon none!' says Dennis O'Neill. Gary Putnam and Debra Petsu agree. So there!

If you think you can do better (and probably can), have a go. If you have friends who think they can do better too, make a race out of the game and the first player to have written out a hundred different words in a composition that makes some sort of sense becomes the winner.

Training Shoes...

Peculiar Leader

Despite its name, this game has nothing to do with politics. It is a parlour game in which you as the Leader get up and tell the other players what you do and don't like. Whenever one of the players feels he has caught on to the reason *why* you like this but you don't like that, he puts up his hand and gives an example of what he thinks you do and don't like. If he has indeed caught onto the gist of your peculiar likes and dislikes, congratulate him. The last player to put up his hand and show he has grasped the nature of your likes and dislikes is the loser. (He's the one who has to do the washing up after the party's over!)

See now how long it takes you to discover why one thing is liked and another disliked in this list of examples:

I like coffee but I don't like tea.
I like trees but I don't like flowers.
I like yellow but I don't like blue.
I like balloons but I don't like party hats.
I like butterflies but I don't like moths.
I like bees but I don't like wasps.
I like slippers but I don't like shoes.
I like the *Express* but I don't like the *Mail*.
I like spoons but I don't like forks.
I like doors but I don't like windows.
I like glasses but I don't like monocles.
I like Trollope but I don't like Dickens.
I like swimmers but I don't like divers.
I like football but I don't like boxing.

As you no doubt guessed by the second or third example, the items 'I liked' included in their spelling the same two vowels or consonants side by side.

Here is a different set of likes and dislikes, this one perhaps more difficult to catch on to than the last:

I like wasps but I don't like bees.
I like the stupid but I don't like the wise.
I like what I am but I don't like what you are.
I like French beans but I don't like peas.
I like noses but I don't like eyes.
I like sheep but I don't like ewes.
I like hard work but I don't like ease.
I like the Avon but I don't like the Dee.
I like lakes but I don't like the sea.
I like the blackbird but I don't like the jay.
I like shopping but I don't like queues.
I like coffee but I don't like tea.
I like me but I don't like you.

Here are all the things 'I didn't like' sounded like letters of the alphabet: Bs, Ys, UR, Ps, Is, Us, Es, D, C, J, Qs, T, U.

When playing the game with a group of three or more, the loser of one round should be the leader of the next and should think up his own formula for what he likes and dislikes.

Questions! Questions!

This is an entertaining game for two players who simply have to fire questions at one another. The first player begins with a question, his opponent must reply with another question, the first player puts a third question, the opponent responds with a fourth, until one of the players falters or forgets himself and fails to ask a question. Repetition is not allowed.

To give you a better idea of how the game can go, here is a brief bout between Adam and Eve:

ADAM What time is it?
EVE Why do you want to know?
ADAM Why do you ask that?
EVE Why can't you answer a civil question?
ADAM Why can't you look at your watch?
EVE When are you going to get yourself a watch?
ADAM What's that got to do with it?
EVE Who do you think you are talking to me like that?
ADAM Where can I find someone who will tell me the time?
EVE Where can I find a husband who can afford a watch of his own?
ADAM When do you stop nagging?
EVE Why don't you stop going on like this?
ADAM Do you know nothing?
EVE What?
ADAM Do you know who you remind me of?
EVE Who?
ADAM Your mother!

Well, he managed to get his insult in, but he lost the game. If you want to see how the game can be played at its most brilliant get hold of a copy of Tom Stoppard's play *Rosencrantz and Guildenstern Are Dead*. The two characters play the game in the play and do so with wit and breathtaking verve.

Starting Point

This is a paper-and-pencil game for one. You begin by writing any word of your choosing on the middle of a blank piece of paper. You then give yourself ten minutes in which to build up a series of other words based on the starting word. The words must not only be physically linked to one another, they must also be broadly related to the theme set by the starting word. Here is an example in which the starting word is ENTERTAINMENT:

```
        A
        MIME
        P
        ORCHESTRA
        I
BALLE T                      CHORUS
        H                    A
    CINEMA                   BAND
        A                    A
    CURTAIN                  RECORDIN G
        R                    E        R
        ENTERT AINMENT                A        F
                C                     MUSICAL
                T                     A        O        S
        CONCERTO                      P        OVER TURE
                R                     H        R        A
                                      O        S        R
                                      N        H
                                      E        O
                                               W
```

Twenty words in ten minutes isn't bad going, but the ease or difficulty of the game depends largely on the word you start with. HOLIDAYS, ANIMALS, PASTIMES, and EDUCATION are easy starting words. TAXIDERMIST, FOLLICLE and BATTERY aren't. If you want to cheat you can always start with the word DICTIONARY, in which case every word you choose to add could be said to be in some way linked to it!

Stinkety Pinkety

This is a parlour game in which players take it in turns to offer a lengthy definition that the others must translate into a simple noun modified by a rhyming adjective.

The elementary examples, given as Definition and Answer, are called Stink Pinks and the nouns and adjectives are monosyllabic:

An obese piece of headgear.
A FAT HAT.

A very unmelodious group of singers.
A DIRE CHOIR.

A canine quadruped from an Irish backwater.
A BOG DOG.

A young man who has lost his wits.
A MAD LAD.

A particularly stupid donkey.
A CRASS ASS.

Stinky Pinkies call for nouns and adjectives of two syllables:

A rather too revealing item of night attire.
A FLIGHTY NIGHTIE.

A foolish fellow called William.
A SILLY BILLY.

An enthusiastic and devoted slave.
A FERVENT SERVANT.

The uppermost part of the house that won't even move in an earthquake.
A STATIC ATTIC.

A pantomime horse.
A PHONEY PONY.

   The really difficult ones are those calling for trisyllabic nouns and adjectives. They are the real Stinkety Pinketies:

A man both arty and austere.
AN AESTHETIC ASCETIC.

A washing-up powder that takes over the world.
AN INSURGENT DETERGENT.

A cactus in a bad mood.
A TRUCULENT SUCCULENT.

A member of the audience who is also someone who has made out a will.
A SPECTATRIX TESTATRIX.

A very dull work of art produced by joining together minute pieces of glass and stone.
A PROSAIC MOSAIC.

It is a gloriously silly game but much more challenging to master than it appears.

Word Chain

Here is a game for two or more in which the players take it in turn to think of a two- or three-word phrase the first word of which *must rhyme* with the last word of the previous player's phrase. The opening player's first phrase is always 'Word chain'.

To give you an idea of the game in action, here is a brief two-handed bout between Adam and Eve. Adam starts:

> ADAM Word chain
> EVE Pane of glass
> ADAM Class of four
> EVE Door handle
> ADAM Candle wax
> EVE Tax the rich
> ADAM Pitch your tent
> EVE Bent double
> ADAM Trouble brewing
> EVE Stewing prunes

At this point Adam gives up because he cannot think of a rhyme for 'prunes'. Eve has won the round and it is her turn to start the next round, again with the opening phrase 'Word chain'.

How many rounds make up a match depends entirely on how much the players enjoy the game. Some people have been known to play the game once and once only: others to have carried on playing for six hours at a stretch! What constitutes a legitimate rhyme and an acceptable phrase must also be left to the commonsense and the whim of the individual players.

As well as being an excellent game for two or more, Word Chain as a mental exercise indulged in on one's own is a perfect cure for insomnia.

Word Endings

Give all players a long list of word endings and let them race to see which one can be the first to find words that end with the given endings. You don't need to make the endings too obscure: the last three letters of a word invariably look a little unfamiliar when they are given without anything preceding them and endings that are very rare tend to slow down the game. Here are some examples of the types of ending that work well:

−don	−ask
−ppy	−ngs
−est	−ity
−ant	−yth
−per	−eth
−the	−ket
−mum	−ssy
−ion	−nge

And here are complete words to match those endings:

abandon	flask
happy	beginnings
best	eternity
errant	myth

wallpaper	brandreth
scythe	market
minimum	messy
ammunition	hinge

In the event of a tie, with two players declaring that they have completed their lists at the very same moment, the player whose list contains the *longer* words is declared the winner.

Words within Words

To play this game all you have to do is take a word – any word will do – and form a list of as many other words as you can think of that are formed from the letters in the given word. For example, out of an everyday word like PEARS you will be surprised to find you can form at least eighteen other words. Here goes: pear, pea, par, pa, pare, ear, are, ape, apse, asp, tab, rape, reap, sap, spear, spare, spa.

Traditionally, only respectable words you could expect to find in a good standard dictionary are allowed, but if you want to add spice to the exercise and increase the game's potential you can always make up your own rules and allow archaic words (such as SAR, the obsolete word for the sea bream), foreign words (such as the Latin ARS), vulgar words (such as the Latin ARS with an E on the end) and plurals (which will almost double the number on the list).

Short words, like PEARS, make for a short game. Here is a selection of longer words with which to start the game. Each one is capable of forming over 50 other words.

saraband	eminence	frightfully
generalization	hypermetropia	machicolate
perspicacious	subjunctive	accidentally
clairvoyance	catastrophe	accomplishment
countrified	euphemistic	passionately
spontaneously	endeavouring	declaration

fantastical	enthronization	corpulence
hamshackle	logarithm	undertaker
oddments	permissible	worryingly

To play the game as a form of solitaire, just choose your word and start scribbling. To play it as a game for two or more, give everyone the same word and the same amount of time and see which player manages to come up with the longest list of legitimate words.

Word Puzzles

For answers see p.213

Puzzling Words

1 There are two English words that contain the five vowels A E I O U once only in their alphabetical order. Can you think of them?

2 There are three English words that contain the five vowels A E I O U once and once only in their reverse alphabetical order (U O I E A). Can you think of them?

3 There is unquestionably an everyday English word that contains the five vowels and the letter Y. What is it?

4 There is a nine-letter English word that contains only one vowel. Can you think of it?

5 There is a fifteen-letter word in which no letter is used more than once. Can you think of it?

6 You will find a word containing six consecutive consonants near Harrods, the department store in London. Can you name it? And can you think of any other words in which six consonants appear consecutively?

7 There is a seven-letter word (plural) which does not include any of the five vowels. Can you think of it?

8 There is a common English word that has 15 letters in it. Five of those letters are the same vowel and the word contains no other vowels. Can you think of it?

9 There is a 16-letter everyday English word in which only one vowel is made use of. What is the word?

10 There are two words that contain the first six letters of the alphabet and yet are only eight letters long. What are the two words?

11   A toddler could make good use of a word with the letters SHCH grouped together in the middle of it. What is the word?

12   There is a word which contains three pairs of identical letters, each pair coming directly after the one before. Can you think of the word?

13   What is the longest word you could play using the right notes in an octave (C, D, E, F, G, A, B, C), given that hyphenated words aren't allowed?

14   Take the letters ERGRO, add three letters to the front and the same three letters in the same order to the rear and you have an everyday English word. What is it?

15   There is an English word in which the letter 'I' appears seven times and which contains no other vowels. Can you think of it?

16   Here are nine words with something important in common: brandy, chastens, craters, grangers, pirated, scampi, stores, swingers, tramps. What do the nine words have in common?

17   There is a word which indicates a good deal of anxiety which runs to fifteen letters and which can be written in longhand without having to go above or below the line. Can you think of it?

18   There is a word that gives an air of being true that contains 14 letters and in which vowels and consonants alternate. Can you think of it?

19   There is an incomprehensible English word that makes
sense and contains eight syllables. Can you think of it?

20   There is a revolutionary English word that contains all
five vowels and the letter Y. Can you think of it?

Puzzling Anagrams

Here are four poems. The blanks in each one can be filled in
with different four-letter words. In each poem the same four
letters can be used to form the different four-letter words. As
poetry the verses may not amount to much. As puzzles, they
are rather ingenious.

1   Landlord, fill the flowing . . . .
    Until the . . . . run over;
    Tonight we . . . . upon the . . . .
    Tomorrow go to Dover!

2   No . . . . was there with cheerful light;
    The . . . . raced round the ship all night;
    With . . . . and wiles the sailors sought,
    But by the . . . . not one was caught.

3   The cook is old, with hoary head,
    His years are quite a . . . . 'tis said.
    Among the . . . . he . . . . away;
    His task is quite a . . . . we'd say.

4   A . . . . old woman, with . . . . intent,
    Put on her . . . . and away she went.
    'Oh, ...,' she cried, 'give me today
    Something on which to . . . , I pray.'

5   Turn each of these words into another word:

ACHE	HEWN	QUIET
ARID	HINGE	SHEET
ASIDE	JAUNT	STRIPES
CAUSE	KALE	UNITE
CITED	LACES	USE
CARTEL	LILTS	VEAL
DAZE	METEOR	VASE
DENIED	NIGHT	WONT
FINGER	OUGHT	WIDER
GIRTH	QUOTE	WENT

6   Turn each of these words into two other words:

AIDS	ETHER
ALES	FARES
ANGEL	ITSELF
BEARD	LAME
BELOW	PINES
BLEATS	PAWS
CHASTE	PEST
DARE	SAINT
DEALER	TIRES
DETAIL	WARDS
EARTH	

7   Turn each of these words into three other words:

AMEN	HARES
COINS	INKS
DIET	MATE
EMIT	PARTS
GLARE	PASTE

8 Turn each of these words into four other words:

ABETS NOTES

ASTER PARES

DRAPES SKATE

9 Turn SCRAPE into five other words.

10 Turn ROAST MULE into one word and ROAST MULES into another word.

Missing Letters

1 To help you observe the Ten Commandments at all times, learn this couplet. To understand it, you will have to add a certain letter to it a certain number of times. Can you do it?

PRSVRYPRFCTMN
VRKPTHSPRCPTSTN

2 Add one letter to this sequence eleven times and you will get a sentence that might be apt were the English Test Eleven playing the Indians in Calcutta:

IEMEFAEDIIEIIGS

3 To make a charmingly alliterative sentence out of this sequence of letters, you will need to add another letter several times:

ALHOUGHHEWOOSIEREDHEYOLD
HEOFOLDALE

4   You will get a lunatic sentence by adding one letter to this sequence five times:

ADENIICANDOCK

Lewis Carroll's Doublets

In 1879, Lewis Carroll wrote a letter to *Vanity Fair* introducing a new kind of puzzle:

The rules of the Puzzle are simple enough. Two words are proposed of the same length; and the Puzzle consists in linking these together by interposing other words, each of which shall differ from the next word *in one letter only*. That is to say, one letter may be changed in one of the given words, then one letter in the word so obtained, and so on, till we arrive at the other given word. The letters must not be interchanged among themselves, but each must keep to its own place. As an example, the word 'head' may be changed into 'tail' by interposing the words 'heal, teal, tell, tall'. I call the two words 'a Doublet', the interposed words 'Links' and the entire series 'a Chain', of which I here append an example: HEAD – heal – teal – tell – tall – TAIL. It is perhaps, needless to state that it is *de rigueur* that the links should be English words, such as might be used in good society.

Now you know how the puzzle works, have a go at these ones which have been set for you by Lewis Carroll himself:

1   Drive PIG into STY with four links.
2   Raise FOUR to FIVE with six links.
3   Make WHEAT into BREAD with six links.
4   Touch CHIN with NOSE with five links.
5   Change TEARS into SMILE with five links.

6   Make HARE into SOUP with six links.
7   PITCH TENTS with five links.
8   Cover EYE with LID with three links.
9   Prove PITY to be GOOD with six links.
10 Turn POOR into RICH with five links.
11 Get WOOD from TREE with seven links.
12 Prove GRASS to be GREEN with seven links.
13 Evolve MAN from APE with five links.
14 Make FLOUR into BREAD with five links.
15 Change ELM into OAK with seven links.
16 Make TEA HOT with three links.
17 Get COAL from MINE with five links.
18 Change BLACK to WHITE with six links.
19 Turn WITCH into FAIRY with twelve links.
20 Make WINTER SUMMER with thirteen links.

Word Squares

A word square is, as you might expect, a square of words. The same word forms the first line and the first column, the same word forms the second line and the second column, the same word forms the third line and the third column, like this:

TOT
OUR
TRY

Constructing squares with three-letter words is easy. Making them out of four-, five- and even six-letter words isn't difficult. The problems really begin to present themselves when you attempt seven-letter word squares, but here is a fine example to show how it can be done:

```
N  E  S  T  L  E  S
E  N  T  R  A  N  T
S  T  R  A  N  G  E
T  R  A  I  T  O  R
L  A  N  T  E  R  N
E  N  G  O  R  G  E
S  T  E  R  N  E  R
```

1 In this puzzle the challenge is to complete the seven-letter word square. To help you, the words for the first two lines and columns are already given and there are clues for the other five words:

```
P  R  E  P  A  R  E
R  E  M  O  D  E  L
E  M  .  .  .  .  .
P  O  .  .  .  .  .
A  D  .  .  .  .  .
R  E  .  .  .  .  .
E  L  .  .  .  .  .
```

Clues

Line and column 3: To imitate zealously, to try to equal or excel
Line and column 4: Controversial discussion
Line and column 5: A thing impenetrably hard
Line and column 6: A train of persons in attendance
Line and column 7: Chosen to office

2   To help you complete this seven-letter word square, you will get no clues, but you will have three of the seven words already in position:

```
M   E   R   G   E   R   S
E   .   .   R   .   .   L
'R   .   .   A   .   .   A
G   R   A   V   I   T   Y
E   .   .   I   .   .   E
R   .   .   T   .   .   R
S   L   A   Y   E   R   S
```

3   This puzzle is based on an impressive nine-letter word square created by Wayne Godwin in Chicago in 1928. To complete it you will need a remarkable vocabulary, as well as the clues and the two words already supplied. REGIMENAL means 'pertaining to a regimen' and EAVESTONE is the name of a town in Yorkshire.

```
.   R   .   .   .   .   .   E   .
R   E   G   I   M   E   N   A   L
.   G   .   .   .   .   .   V   .
.   I   .   .   .   .   .   E   .
.   M   .   .   .   .   .   S   .
.   E   .   .   .   .   .   T   .
.   N   .   .   .   .   .   O   .
E   A   V   E   S   T   O   N   E
.   L   .   .   .   .   .   E   .
```

Clues

Line and column 1: Monastic refectories
Line and column 3: Inclined to agitate
Line and column 4: Minerals containing titanium

Line and column 5: A person who believes in creation by emanation
Line and column 6: To titrate for the second time (and for those who didn't know what 'to titrate' for the first time was, to titrate means 'to determine the quantity of a given constituent in a compound by observing the quantity of a standard solution necessary to convert this constituent into another form'.)
Line and column 7: A person who initiates
Line and column 9: Bedaubed and smeared

Finally, here, not as a puzzle but simply as a phenomenon at which to marvel, is a ten-letter word square, kindly supplied by my friend Darryl Francis, one of Britain's foremost word-smiths. Nine-letter word squares are rareties, but ten-letter ones are almost unheard of. Mr Francis believes this one to be the best of the breed. To enjoy it to the full you need a library of dictionaries and an indulgent nature: you have to forgive the fact that lines and columns 8, 9 and 10 repeat the word in lines and columns 3, 4 and 5. Even so, it is a remarkable achievement:

1	O	R	A	N	G	U	T	A	N	G
2	R	A	N	G	A	R	A	N	G	A
3	A	N	D	O	L	A	N	D	O	L
4	N	G	O	T	A	N	G	O	T	A
5	G	A	L	A	N	G	A	L	A	N
6	U	R	A	N	G	U	T	A	N	G
7	T	A	N	G	A	T	A	N	G	A
3	A	N	D	O	L	A	N	D	O	L
4	N	G	O	T	A	N	G	O	T	A
5	G	A	L	A	N	G	A	L	A	N

Definitions

1 The orangutan: a spelling given by Funk & Wagnalls' *New Standard Dictionary*, published by Funk & Wagnalls, 1946.

2 In the Caroline Islands, a name for parsley fern growing in the cracks of old walls; taken from *The Caroline Islands* by Frederick Christian, published in London in 1899.

3 A Chinese fly, a tincture of which is used as a blistering agent; taken from *An Illustrated Encyclopedic Medical Dictionary* by Frank Foster, published in New York between 1888 and 1894.

4 Town on the western shore of Lake Nyasa, now spelled KOTA KOTA; taken from Longmans' *Gazetteer of the World* by George Chisholm, published in London and New York in 1902.

5 A mountain in Sorsogon Province, on Luzon Island, in the Philippines; taken from *A Pronouncing Gazetteer and Geographical Dictionary of the Philippine Islands*, published by the US War Department, in Washington, in 1902.

6 The Urangutang: a spelling given by the *Oxford English Dictionary*, 1933.

7 A name for the trinity of ancient Peruvian divinities, Pachama, Virakotch and Mamakotcha; taken from *The Reader's Handbook of Allusions, References, Plots and Stories*, by E Cobham Brewer, published in Philadelphia, in 1880.

Toffe nosed...

Word Quizzes

For answers see p.222

What's That?

Here is a series of dictionary definitions. The challenge is to see if you can spot which word is being defined.

1 'A devoted follower'. Of which of these words is that a definition:

ATTENDANT
HANDMAIDEN
ACOLYTE
HENCHMAN

2 'The white milky fluid formed by the action of the pancreatic juice and the bile on the chyme':

BLADDER
CHYLE
ALBUMEN
NECTAR

3 'A soft cake made of flour, beaten egg, milk and barm, mixed into batter, and baked on an iron plate':

PANCAKE
CRUMPET
SPONGE
BAP

4 'Liberation from imprisonment, servitude or political subjection':

AMNESTY
DISENFRANCHISEMENT
SURRENDER
DISENSLAVEMENT

5 'To coagulate, clot, congeal':

FREEZE
CURDLE
SOUR
ACIDIFY

6 'A plant of the genus Pelargonium':

GERANIUM
DAFFODIL
ORCHID
LILAC

7 'Impenetrable, unfathomable, entirely mysterious':

SECRET
IGNORANT
INSENSIBLE
INSCRUTABLE

8 'A reading- or singing-desk in a church':

PODIUM
PLATFORM
PULPIT
LECTERN

9 'A dish made of hulled wheat boiled in milk and seasoned with cinnamon, sugar, etc':

PORRIDGE
YOGHURT
FRUMENTY
TAPIOCA

10 'Derived from the name of a father or ancestor':

PATRONYMIC
SURNAME
NICKNAME
PSEUDONYM

11 'A back door, a private door, any door or gate distinct from the main entrance':

PORTICO
WICKET
POSTERN
REREDOS

12 'A black raucous-voiced European and Asiatic bird nesting in colonies':

RAVEN
CORNCRAKE
EAGLE
ROOK

13 'A fore-and-aft sail, set with a gaff and boom at the aftermost part of the ship':

TOPSAIL
WINDBREAKER
SPANKER
YARDBOROUGH

14 'The science of poisons':

TAXIDERMY
THEOSOPHY
TOXICOLOGY
TRACASSERIE

15 'A combination of three vowel sounds in one syllable':

TONGUETWISTER
TRYST
TRIPHTHONG
TRIPARTITE

16 'Consisting of trimming and clipping shrubs into ornamental or fantastic shapes':

SHRUBBERY
TOPIARY
CAPABILITY
ARBORETUM

17 'A quantic of equation of the sixth degree':

SEXTIC
SEXTILLION
SEXTET
SEXTARY

18 'A quantity of paper, properly 480 sheets':

REAM
QUIRE
BALE
PACK

19 'Cunning thievishness':

BURGLARY
ROBBERY
DECEIT
STEALTH

20 'Showy or gaudy with no real value':

TAWDRY
TATTY
TAURYLIC
TELLUROUS

Spelling Bee

Below is a list of common words that are commonly misspelt.
Here some of them are given with their correct spelling and
some are given with an incorrect spelling. Can you spot the
misspelling?

RHODODENDRON	ACCOMODATE	CASTIGATED
ASSASSINATE	ONOMATOPOEIA	MERRH
CRONOLOGY	FACSIMILE	SOLILOQUY
EMBARRASSMENT	ANNIHILATE	ABSTRACTION
PHENOMENON	HANDFULL	SATELITE
CANTANCKEROUS	FUCHSIA	RECIEPT
DIAPHRAMG	RESUSCITATE	ADJUSTMENT
PNEUMONIA	BIVOUACKING	AQUISITIVE
DISSAPPEAR	PREFERABLE	DISINCLINATION
MAINTENANCE	ADRESS	HARASMENT
DIPTHERIA	MEASUREMENT	INACCESSABLE
RETORIC	OBLOQUY	ARMADILLO
EUFEMISM	PARRALEL	FORSYTHIA
DESPARATE	GRAMAPHONE	NONCHALANT
INFALLIBLE	CHAOTIC	NEBULOUS
COLOSSAL	HYDRANGEA	CONSCIENSIOUS
DIARHOEA	LIQUIFY	ADVANTAGEOUS
CANNIBAL	PICKNICKER	SCINTILLATING
RHUEBARB	PSYCHIATRIST	FLACCID
PRIVILEDGE	EPHEMERAL	CONVALESCENT

Scottish English

The Scots call some very ordinary things some very odd
names. Can you work out the meanings of these Scottish
words?

1 What's a *baillie*?

An advocate
A magistrate
A barrister
A solicitor

2 What's a *bairn*?

A barn
A stream
A coin
A child

3 What's a *biggin*?

A dance
A building
A hill
A bird

4 What's a *bubblyjock*?

A drink
An undergarment
A bad joke
A turkey

5 What are *champit tatties*?

Ragged clothes
A collection of sporrans
Mashed potatoes
Gaelic songs

6 What does *couthy* mean?

Vulgar
Smart
Abusive
Cosy

7 What are *fernitickles*?

Pieces of furniture
Autumn leaves
Colliwobbles
Freckles

8 What is a *gowan*?

An eiderdown
A daisy
A tortoise
A cloak

9 What is a *hoolit*?

A party
A street lamp
An illness
An owl

10 What do you do when you *jalouse*?

Become jealous
Race
Die
Guess

11 What is a *lug*?

A slug
An ear
A journey
A lung

12 What is a *pneb*?

A pen nib
A lake
A butterfly
A nose

13 What is an *oxter*?

An armpit
A bowl of soup
A bullock
A petticoat

14 What is a *puddock*?

A field for grazing
A kind of cheesecake
A bruise
A frog

15 What is a *spirtle*?

A stick for stirring porridge
A stinging nettle
A painting
A poem

16 What is a *tattie bogle*?

A badly dressed ghost
A sack of potatoes
A French horn
A scarecrow

17 What is a *thrapple*?

An argument
A throat
A ship
A kind of crumpet

18 When you are *wabbit* how do you feel?

Exhilarated
Excited
Expectant
Exhausted

19 What is a *whigmaleerie*?

A wedding anniversary
A political party
A Brussels sprout
A trinket

20 What is a *yett*?

A gate
A snowman
A sailing boat
A Scottish funeral

American English

'The English', as Oscar Wilde observed, 'have really everything in common with the Americans, except, of course, language.' Can you work out what each of these American words means?

1 What is a *band-aid*?

An Arts Council grant
A nuclear fall-out shelter
A telephone
An elastoplast

2 What is a *barette*?

A hat
A thermometer
A pushchair
A hairslide

3 What is *bell pepper*?

Black pepper
Red pepper
Green pepper
Salt

4 What is a *billfold*?

A noticeboard
A wallet
A bird's beak
A briefcase

5 What is a *caravan*?

A caravan
A sweet
A tent
A convoy

6 What are *checkers*?

Lavatory attendants
Gambling chips
Draughts
Checked shorts

7 What is a *closet*?

A cupboard
A side entrance
A toilet
A fishing net

8 What is a *comforter*?

A priest
A headscarf
An eiderdown
A teddy bear

9 What is *cream of wheat*?

Porridge
Semolina
Lemon Curd
Tapioca

10 What is *denatured alcohol*?

Vodka
Gin
Martini
Methylated spirits

11 What is a *derby*?

A race
A game
A dog
A bowler hat

12 What is a *diaper*?

A hare
A jewel-box
A nappy
A semi-detached house

13 What is a *faucet*?

An escalator
A pesticide
A pair of pliers
A tap

14 What is a *jelly roll*?

A kind of high-jump
A bank robbery
A Swiss roll
A kind of jam

15 What are *knickers*?

Underpants
Plus-fours
Dollar bills
Thieves

French Window...

16 What is *molasses*?

Black treacle
Fish pâté
A stomach upset
Galoshes

17 What is a *nightstick*?

A torch
A walking stick
A truncheon
An insect

18 What is a *period*?

A chairman
A flyover
A pancake
A full stop

19 What is a *pollywog*?

A doll
A wig
A tadpole
A combine harvester

20 What is *tic-tac-toe*?

The Morse code
Chocolate fudge
Seaweed
The game of noughts
and crosses

Two into One Will Go

Here are 60 three-letter words. By combining the 30 words in
the first column with the 30 words in the second column you
can create 30 six-letter words. Have a go:

CAR	HER
DON	TEE
BUT	ANT
BET	BIT
TEA	SON
DOT	TON
CUR	ATE
COW	LET
FOR	PET
ROT	KEY
HUM	TON
FUR	RAY
NET	POT
RAT	AGE

SEA	FEW
NAP	BOY
SOD	TON
IMP	OUR
OUT	AGE
BAR	ROW
SAT	MAN
OUT	SON
INN	KIN
HAM	DEN
COT	ART
FAT	LAW
SET	IRE
ERR	WIT
TIT	ATE
PAR	HER

What's This?

The easy one

1 What is a *chromatrope*? A deep-sea fish
A lantern slide
A chemical compound
A miner's helmet

2 What is a *diaeresis*? A stomach complaint
A marquee
An ecclesiastical boundary
A mark put over the second of
two vowels

3 What is a *drone*? An ugly woman
An airport
A male honey-bee
A medieval chant

4 What is an *exegesis*?   An outrageous statement
                                   An exposition of the Scriptures
                                   A three-humped camel
                                   A Latin benediction

5 What is *felicide*?   The writing of epic poetry
                                   The juice of poisonous herbs
                                   The killing of cats
                                   Having more than two wives at
                                   the same time

6 What is *fission*?   The killing of whales
                                   The division of cells
                                   The ejecting of phlegm
                                   The lancing of boils

7 What is a *gingko*?   A lizard
                                   A coin
                                   A tree
                                   A band-leader

8 What is a *jalousie*?   A kind of nervous hysteria
                                   A kind of shutter or blind
                                   A kind of nightdress
                                   A kind of warming-pan

9 What is a *lory*?   A small van
                                   A spiritual text
                                   A parrot-like bird
                                   An aardvark's young

10 What is a *marmoset*?   A kind of marmalade
                                   A kind of porcupine
                                   A kind of Indian guru
                                   A kind of monkey

11 What is a *missel*?

A prayer book
A thrush
A rocket
A small alley

12 What is an *olio*?

A mixed dish
A Burmese sergeant
A part of an altar
A safety belt

13 What is an *orfe*?

A goldfish
A flat-bottomed boat
A small island
A foul smell

14 What is a *peritoneum*?

A baritone singer
A headstone in a graveyard
A part of the stomach
A eulogy

15 What is a *piastre*?

A Spanish silver coin
A German sheep dog
An Italian pastry
A Portuguese public square

16 What is *potable*?

Something you can carry easily
Something made of pottery
Something you can drink
Something you can find on the beach

17 What is a *privet*?

A rank in the Irish army
An Elizabethan lavatory
A bushy evergreen shrub
A dessert

18 What is a *punnet*?

Someone who makes puns
A fan
Part of the engine of a car
A basket for fruit

19 What is *roup*?

A kind of acid
A kind of tax
A kind of poultry disease
A kind of sweet potato

20 What is a *zephyr*?

An African animal
A wind
An uncut diamont
An operation performed on the throat

What's This?

The not-so-easy one

1 What is a *bosset*?

A small man
A small protuberance
A small hedge
A small bowl for medicine

2 What is a *chrematist*?

Someone who runs a crematorium
Someone who studies fossils
Someone who studies wealth
Someone who invents electronic devices

3 What is a *clypeole*?

A saucer
A shield
A muscle
A clay pigeon

4 What is a *foumart*?

A pastry
A polecat
A fairground
A birth mark

5 What is a *funambulist*?

A fakir
A rope walker
A collector of precious metals
A believer in the literal story of
the Bible

6 What is a *gawk*?

A hunting bird
An awkward person
A part of the spine
A South American fieldmouse

7 What is a *homuncle*?

A distant relative
A kind of tobacco
A Persian rug
A little man

8 What is a *joskin*?

A leather cloak
A country bumpkin
A ship's anchor
A dish of mixed herbs

9 What is a *manatee*?

A golf course
A sun hat
A sea cow
A sword swallower

10 What is a *monticule*?

Part of the fingernail
A small hill
A priest's hole
A case for carrying surgical
instruments

11 What is a *natterjack*?

A linguist
A blueberry
A moth
A toad

12 What is a *noyau*?

A liqueur of brandy
A vision of the Virgin Mary
A death by drowning
A reef knot

13 What is an *onager*?

Syrup of figs
A wild ass
A noise made by a dying swan
A petty thief or pickpocket

14 What is *pabulum*?

Silk
Food
Part of the brain
The key to a chastity belt

15 What is a *pousette*?

A form of dancing
A type of green bean
A kind of mental telepathy
A small wheel-chair

16 What is a *pratincole*?

A false window
A bird
A joint
Part of the spine of a book

17 What is a
psilanthropist?

Someone who gives away large
sums of money
Someone who collects rare
species of marsupials
Someone who believes that
Christ was an ordinary mortal
Someone who has a terminal
illness and does not know it

18 What is *realgar*?

Arsenic
Ozone
Wallpaper
Seventeenth-century German
music

19 What is *smallage*?

Rotting refuse
A ship's kitchen
A wild celery
Coconut matting

20 What is *zygoma*?

The belief in one's own
infallibility
Part of the cheek
A carnivorous quadruped
A fantastical daydream

Solutions to the Word Puzzles

Puzzling Words

1 Abstemious. Facetious.
2 Uncomplimentary, unnoticeably, subcontinental.
3 Unquestionably!
4 Strengths.
5 Uncopyrightable. Dermatoglyphics and misconjugatedly are less obvious, but equally acceptable.
6 Knightsbridge is the name of the street in which Harrods is situated. Among possible words are: archchronicler, catchphrase, latchstring and lengthsmen.
7 Rhythms.
8 Defencelessness.
9 Strengthlessness.
10 Boldface. Feedback.
11 Pushchair.
12 Book-keeper.
13 Bebedded, bedeafed, cabbaged, debagged and debadged are five possibilities.
14 Underground.
15 Indivisibilities.
16 All the words in the list can be reduced by one letter at a time and still form complete words. For example:

BRANDY	CHASTENS	CRATERS
BRAND	CHASTEN	CRATER
BRAN	CHASTE	CRATE
RAN	HASTE	RATE
AN	HAST	ATE
A	HAS	AT
	AS	A
	A	

17 Overnervousness.
18 Verisimilitude.
19 Incomprehensibility.
20 Revolutionary!

Puzzling Anagrams

1 Landlord, fill the flowing pots,
   Until the tops run over;
   Tonight we stop upon the post,
   Tomorrow go to Dover.

2 No star was there with cheerful light;
   The rats raced round the ship all night;
   With arts and wiles and sailors sought,
   But by the tars not one was caught.

3 The cook is old with hoary head,
   His years are quite a span, 'tis said.
   Among the pans he naps away;
   His talk is quite a snap we'd say.

4 A vile old woman, with evil intent.
   Put on her veil and away she went.
   'Oh, Levi,' she cried, 'give me today
   Something on which to live, I pray.'

5 ACHE: EACH   LILTS: STILL

   ARID: RAID   METEOR: REMOTE

   ASIDE: IDEAS   NIGHT: THING

   CAUSE: SAUCE   OUGHT: TOUGH

   CITED: EDICT   QUOTE: TOQUE

   CARTEL: CLARET   QUIET: QUITE

   DAZE: ADZE   SHEET: THESE

   DENIED: INDEED   STRIPES: PERSIST

FINGER: FRINGE

GIRTH: RIGHT

HEWN: WHEN

HINGE: NEIGH

JAUNT: JUNTA

KALE: LAKE

LACES: SCALE

UNITE: UNTIE

USE: SUE

VEAL: VALE

VASE: SAVE

WONT: TOWN

WIDER: WEIRD

WENT: NEWT

6   AIDS: SAID; DAIS
    ALES: SALE, SEAL
    ANGEL: ANGLE, GLEAN
    BEARD: BARED, BREAD
    BELOW: BOWEL, ELBOW
    BLEATS: STABLE, TABLES
    CHASTE: CHEATS, SCATHE
    DARE: DEAR, READ
    DEALER: LEADER, REDEAL
    DETAIL: DILATE, TAILED
    EARTH: HEART, HATER
    ETHER: THERE, THREE
    FARES: FEARS, SAFER
    ITSELF: STIFLE, FILETS
    LAME: MALE, MEAL
    PINES: SPINE, SNIPE
    PAWS: SWAP, WASP
    PEST: PETS, STEP
    SAINT: SATIN, STAIN
    TIRES: TRIES, RITES
    WARDS: SWARD, DRAWS

7   AMEN: NAME, MANE, MEAN
    COINS: ICONS, SCION, SONIC
    DIET: EDIT, TIDE, TIED
    EMIT: ITEM, MITE, TIME
    GLARE: LAGER, LARGE, REGAL
    HARES: HEARS, SHARE, SHEAR
    INKS: KINS, SINK, SKIN
    MATE: MEAT, TAME, TEAM
    PARTS: STRAP, SPRAT, TRAPS
    PASTE: PATES, TAPES

8 ABETS: BATES, BASTE, BEAST, BEATS
   ASTER: RATES, STARE, TARES, TEARS
   DRAPES: PARSED, SPADER, SPARED, SPREAD
   NOTES: ONSET, SETON, STONE, TONES
   PARES: PEARS, REAPS, RAPES, SPARE
   SKATE: STAKE, STEAK, TEAKS, TAKES

9 SCRAPE: CAPERS, CRAPES, PACERS,
   RECAPS, SPACER

10 ROAST MULE: EMULATORS
    ROAST MULES: SOMERSAULT

Missing Letters

1 The missing letter is *E* and this is the couplet:

   Persevere ye perfect men,
   Ever keep these precepts ten.

2 The missing letter is *N* and this is the sentence:

   Nine men fanned in nine innings.

3 The missing letter is *T* and this is the alliterative
   sentence:

   Although the two tots tittered, they told
   the oft-told tale.

4 The missing letter is *M* and this is the sentence:

Mad men mimic and mock.

Lewis Carroll's Doublets

1 PIG   WAG   SAY
   WIG   WAY   STY

2 FOUR   FOOT   FIRE
   FOUL   FORT   FIVE
   FOOL   FORE

3 WHEAT   CHEEP   BREED
   CHEAT   CREEP   BREAD
   CHEAP   CREED

4 nose   core   coin
   note   corn   chin
   cote

5 tears   stare   stile
   sears   stale   smile
   stars

6 hare   sack   soap
   hark   sock   soup
   hack   soak

7 pitch   wench   tenth
   pinch   tench   tents
   winch

8	EYE	DIE	LID
	DYE	DID	

9	PITY	FINS	FOOD
	PITS	FIND	GOOD
	PINS	FOND	

10	POOR	ROOK	RICK
	BOOR	ROCK	RICH
	BOOK		

11	TREE	FLED	WELD
	FREE	FEED	WOLD
	FLEE	WEED	WOOD

12	GRASS	TRESS	FREED
	CRASS	TREES	GREED
	CRESS	FREES	GREEN

13	APE	ERR	MAR
	ARE	EAR	MAN
	ERE		

14	FLOUR	BLOOD	BROAD
	FLOOR	BROOD	BREAD
	FLOOD		

15	ELM	AIL	FAR
	ELL	AIR	OAR
	ALL	FIR	OAK

16	TEA	SET	HOT
	SEA	SOT	

17	MINE	MOST	COAT
	MINT	MOAT	COAL
	MIST		

18	BLACK	CLINK	WHINE
	BLANK	CHINK	WHITE
	BLINK	CHINE	

19	WITCH	TENTS	FALLS
	WINCH	TINTS	FAILS
	WENCH	TILTS	FAIRS
	TENCH	TILLS	FAIRY
	TENTH	FILLS	

20	WINTER	HARDER	DAMMED
	WINNER	HARPER	DIMMED
	WANNER	HAMPER	DIMMER
	WANDER	DAMPER	SIMMER
	WARNER	DAMPED	SUMMER

It should be noted that several of these Doublets can in fact be accomplished with fewer links than Lewis Carroll realized.

Word Squares

1

P	R	E	P	A	R	E
R	E	M	O	D	E	L
E	M	U	L	A	T	E
P	O	L	E	M	I	C
A	D	A	M	A	N	T
R	E	T	I	N	U	E
E	L	E	C	T	E	D

2

M	E	R	G	E	R	S
E	T	E	R	N	A	L
R	E	G	A	T	T	A
G	R	A	V	I	T	Y

```
E  N  T  I  T  L  E
R  A  T  T  L  E  R
S  L  A  Y  E  R  S

3     F  R  A  T  E  R  I  E  S
      R  E  G  I  M  E  N  A  L
      A  G  I  T  A  T  I  V  E
      T  I  T  A  N  I  T  E  S
      E  M  A  N  A  T  I  S  T
      R  E  T  I  T  R  A  T  E
      I  N  I  T  I  A  T  O  R
      E  A  V  E  S  T  O  N  E
      S  L  E  S  T  E  R  E  D
```

Answers to the Word Quizzes

What's That?

1	ACOLYTE	11	POSTERN
2	CHYLE	12	ROOK
3	CRUMPET	13	SPANKER
4	DISENFRANCHISEMENT	14	TOXICOLOGY
5	CURDLE	15	TRIPHTHONG
6	GERANIUM	16	TOPIARY
7	INSCRUTABLE	17	SEXTIC
8	LECTERN	18	REAM
9	FRUMENTY	19	STEALTH
10	PATRONYMIC	20	TAWDRY

Spelling Bee

Twenty-five of the words in the list were given with incorrect spellings. Here they are, with their spelling corrected:

CHRONOLOGY	ADDRESS
CANTANKEROUS	PARALLEL
DIAPHRAGM	GRAMOPHONE
DISAPPEAR	LIQUEFY
RHETORIC	PICNICKER
EUPHEMISM	MYRRH
DESPERATE	SATELLITE
DIARRHOEA	RECEIPT
RHUBARB	ACQUISITIVE
PRIVILEGE	HARASSMENT
ACCOMMODATE	INACCESSIBLE
HANDFUL	CONSCIENTIOUS

Scottish English

1 A magistrate
2 A child
3 A building
4 A turkey
5 Mashed potatoes
6 Cosy
7 Freckles
8 A daisy
9 An owl
10 Guess
11 An ear
12 A nose
13 An armpit
14 A frog
15 A stick for stirring porridge
16 A scarecrow
17 A throat
18 Exhausted
19 A trinket
20 A gate

American English

1 An elastoplast
2 A hairslide
3 Green pepper
4 A wallet
5 A convoy
6 Draughts
7 A cupboard
8 An eiderdown
9 Semolina
10 Methylated spirits
11 A bowler hat
12 A nappy

13 A tap
14 A Swiss roll
15 Plus fours
16 Black treacle
17 A truncheon
18 A full stop
19 A tadpole
20 The game of noughts and crosses.

Two into One Will Go

CARPET	NAPKIN
DONKEY	SODDEN
BUTTON	IMPART
BETRAY	OUTLAW
TEAPOT	BARMAN
DOTAGE	SATIRE
CURFEW	OUTWIT
COWBOY	INNATE
FORAGE	HAMLET
ROTTEN	COTTON
HUMOUR	FATHER
FURROW	SETTEE
NETHER	ERRANT
RATHER	TITBIT
SEASON	PARSON

What's This?

The easy one

1 A lantern slide
2 A mark put over the second of two vowels
3 A male honey-bee

4 An exposition of the Scriptures
5 The killing of cats
6 The division of cells
7 A tree
8 A kind of shutter or blind
9 A parrot-like bird
10 A kind of monkey
11 A thrush
12 A mixed dish
13 A goldfish
14 A part of the stomach
15 A Spanish silver coin
16 Something you can drink
17 A bushy evergreen shrub
18 A basket for fruit
19 A kind of poultry disease
20 A wind

What's This?

The not-so-easy one

1 A small protuberance
2 Someone who studies wealth
3 A shield
4 A polecat
5 A rope walker
6 An awkward person
7 A little man
8 A country bumpkin
9 A sea cow
10 A small hill
11 A toad
12 A liqueur of brandy
13 A wild ass

14 Food
15 A form of dancing
16 A bird
17 Someone who believes that Christ was an ordinary mortal
18 Arsenic
19 A wild celery
20 Part of the cheek

Bibliography

Bombaugh, C C, *Oddities and Curiosities of Words and Literature*, edited and annotated by Martin Gardner, Dover Publications, New York, 1961.

Brown, Ivor, *A Word in Your Ear*, Cape, 1942, and revised edition 1953.

Dillard, J L, *All-American English*, Random House, New York, 1975. *Dictionary of Mnemonics*, Eyre Methuen, 1972.

Espy Willard, *An Almanac of Words at Play*, Clarkson N Potter, New York, 1975.

Fowler, H W, *Modern English Usage*, revised by Sir Ernest Gowers, Oxford University Press, 1968.

Fowler H W and F G, *The King's English*, third edition, Oxford University Press, 1968.

Gowers, Sir Ernest, *The Complete Plain Words*, revised by Sir Bruce Fraser, H M Stationery Office, 1973.

Miller, Casey, and Swift, Kate, *Words and Women*, Victor Gollancz, 1977.

Partridge, Eric, *Usage and Abusage*, Hamish Hamilton, 1947.

Partridge, Eric, *The Dictionary of Slang and Unconventional English*, abridged by Jacqueline Simpson, Penguin Books, 1972.

Pei, Mario, *Words in Sheep's Clothing*, George Allen & Unwin, 1970.

Ridout, Ronald, and Witting, Clifford, *The Facts of English* Revised by Ronald Ridout and Anthony Hern, Pan Books, 1973.

Shipley, Joseph T, *In Praise of English*, Times Books, New York, 1977.

Sperling, Susan Kelz, *Poplollies and Bellibones*, Clarkson N Potter, New York, 1977.

Wood, Frederick, *Current English Usage*, Macmillan, 1962.